Mo

MW01255051

"The separation of prophetic and pastoral preaching: gone. No more _____ ____ ___ week after to week to different purposes of the sermon. Drawing on the scholarship of critical pedagogy, Voelz revives and revises the traditional understanding of the preacher-as-teacher in ways that will transform your preaching into being transformative."
—O. Wesley Allen Jr., Lois Craddock Perkins Professor of Homiletics, Perkins School of Theology, Dallas, TX

"I have long believed that theological illiteracy is at the heart of the current struggles of the long-established churches. Richard Voelz points to the teaching dimension of preaching as a way of energizing the contemporary church."
—Ronald J. Allen, Professor of Preaching, and Gospels and Letters, Emeritus, Christian Theological Seminary, Indianapolis, IN

"What excites me about this book is the way it helps clergy approach controversial public issues in the pulpit by using critical pedagogy to teach critical thinking. This book will have immediate relevancy in our age of contentious politics and lend itself to practical application for today's preachers. I plan to use this book in my seminary classes and recommend it for practicing preachers."
—Leah D. Schade, assistant professor of preaching and worship, Lexington Theological Seminary, Lexington, KY

"Voelz shows preachers how to teach their congregations to think critically and deeply about the world in which they live. But for Voelz, critical thinking must be accompanied by a radical imagination that reaches beyond the current social and political situations and circumstances of the world to the myriad possibilities extant in the kingdom of God. Teaching people to think critically about the world can empower many who have been mis-educated by dominant pedagogy to live and move within prescribed boundaries, to instead transgress, expand, or even eliminate boundaries by igniting their ability to hope and then strive to realize the possibilities of that hope."
—Debra J. Mumford, Frank H. Caldwell Professor of Homiletics, Louisville Presbyterian Theological Seminary, Louisville, KY

"Building on the ideas of Paulo Friere and Henry Giroux, this book opens up a new perspective on the preacher as teacher."
—John S. McClure, Charles G. Finney Professor of Preaching and Worship, Vanderbilt Divinity School, Nashville, TN

Other Books in the Artistry of Preaching Series

Preaching as Poetry: Beauty, Goodness, and Truth in Every Sermon
by Paul Scott Wilson

Actuality: Real Life Stories for Sermons That Matter
by Scott Hoezee

Preaching in Pictures: Using Images for Sermons That Connect
by Peter Jonker

Preaching with Empathy: Crafting Sermons in a Callous Culture
by Lenny Luchetti

Words That Heal: Preaching Hope to Wounded Souls
by Joni S. Sancken

The Artistry of Preaching Series

Preaching to Teach

Inspire People to Think and Act

Richard Voelz

Abingdon Press

Nashville

PREACHING TO TEACH:
INSPIRE PEOPLE TO THINK AND ACT

Copyright © 2019 by Abingdon Press

Library of Congress Cataloging-in-Publication Data has been requested.

978-1-5018-6807-8

19 20 21 22 23 24 25 26 27 28—10 9 8 7 6 5 4 3 2 1
MANUFACTURED IN THE UNITED STATES OF AMERICA

To the memory of my father,

David Durham Voelz Sr.,

who loved Christ's church.

Husband, Father, Grandfather,

and tireless supporter

July 27, 1949–May 24, 2017

*The Lord G*OD *has given me
the tongue of a teacher,
that I may know how to sustain
the weary with a word.*

Isaiah 50:4 (NRSV)

Contents

Series Preface

The Artistry of Preaching series gives practical guidance on matters that receive insufficient attention in preaching literature yet are key for preachers who seek greater creative expression in their preaching. Fresh, faithful proclamation requires imagination and creative engagement of the Bible and our world. There is no shortage of commentaries on the Bible and books on biblical interpretation for preaching, but there is a shortage of practical resources to help strengthen the creativity of preachers to facilitate their proclamation of the gospel.

The first volume of this series, *Preaching as Poetry: Beauty, Goodness, and Truth in Every Sermon*, redefines preaching for our current postmodern age. The world has changed. Beauty, goodness, and truth no longer mean what they used to mean as fixed absolute and universal standards. While this may be threatening to some preachers, the new meanings can actually allow preachers fresh and creative ways to proclaim God's love and saving purposes in a rapidly changing world. Preaching needs to be reconceived as a kind of poetry, in the sense of communicating the wondrous beauty of God's saving purposes and promises in troubled times. God needs to be presented in terms of experience and relationships, more than abstractions, and faith needs to be presented as something that adds beauty, goodness, and truth to life. In other words, for a new generation that seeks concrete outcomes and immediate benefits, faith needs to be presented as a relationship with God and neighbor that affords deep meaning and great joy.

The second volume of the series, *Actuality: Real-Life Stories for Sermons That Matter*, by Scott Hoezee, is a resource for preachers who want guidance to be better storytellers or to use story more effectively to communicate with a new generation. There readers will also find a collection of stories that both preach and stimulate their imaginations to identify stories from their own contexts. Preachers can easily run out of good stories to use that embody the gospel. The problem is not a shortage of stories; they are all around in everyday events. The task is learning how to harvest them, as will be shown here. Preachers long for good stories, and today's listeners are not content with the canned internet illustrations that sound artificial and have a predictable moral. Rather they want stories rooted in the actual world in which they live, that depict life as they know it, and that can function as Jesus's stories did, as parables and metaphors that bear God's grace to their hearers.

The third volume, *Preaching in Pictures: Using Images for Sermons That Connect*, helps preachers add some spark and imagination with a dominant or captivating image. The challenge is not just to find images that are visually evocative; it is to find ones that are artistic, propulsive, and theologically centered. By moving from a theme sentence to an image statement, preachers can move their composition from being a "beautiful mess" to an affective sermon. Preachers can benefit from the book's practical exercises adapted from creative writers and poets that help in the art of selecting images and polishing them for use in relation to biblical texts. Equally important in the current times, readers will find guidance on using images on screens in worship that can powerfully assist the work of the Spirit and increase the joy of preaching.

The fourth volume of The Artistry of Preaching series is *Preaching with Empathy: Crafting Sermons in a Callous Culture* by Lenny Luchetti. Empathy is a subject that some people might not connect with art and artistry. They may think of empathy as a feature of personality, something one either has or does not have. To some degree, they are right. What makes the present volume so remarkable is that Lenny Luchetti teaches the art of putting empathy into practice in preaching. However great or small our natural empathy, it can be enhanced by tending to it.

Empathy is needed for preaching to be transformative for the listeners and society in general. It is not enough for preachers just to know they love their congregations. The congregations must know it. Preachers must show it, ensuring that it is experienced through what is done and said. Empathy must be nurtured and communicated through what one says about the Bible and the world today, and about the various relationships fostered in preaching. While the preacher's love for the people is essential, the goal of empathic homiletical practice is to communicate God's love in Christ and through the Spirit, to enable the people's ministry through empathy for one another. In other words, empathy is a spiritual practice that individual preachers can cultivate and utilize to enhance their sermons, as Luchetti shows and as many have done through history. His volume could not come at a better time, when so much in the current culture seems to point toward apathy. He brings a corrective that is hopeful, practical, encouraging, and inspiring.

Words That Heal: Preaching Hope to Wounded Souls is the fifth volume of the series. In this innovative volume, Joni Sancken develops tools for preachers to speak effectively to people in congregations who carry with them the effects of untended wounds caused by past hurts, brokenness, tragedies, and trauma. These include the effects of sexual or emotional abuse, witnessing violence perhaps in war, or having caused an accident or hurting someone you love. Wounds to the soul, if ignored, can be debilitating and inhibit growth. This volume teaches that there is an art to ministering to soul wounds. Together with the Holy Spirit, preachers can initiate and help participate in a healing process. Not everyone in the pews has suffered trauma, but everyone carries pain. Everyone can benefit from hearing issues named, the truth spoken in love, and words that offer hope. Sancken offers practical tools. She encourages preachers to proclaim what the church uniquely offers: the love, healing grace, and redemptive power of God that emanates from the cross of Christ. This book is about compassionate preaching that not only heals but also restores faithful and joyous community.

In the current volume, *Preaching to Teach*, Richard Voelz does a splendid job of reconceiving preaching in terms of teaching. Drawing on current educational and social theory, preaching becomes the action of radically and prophetically re-imagining the world to conform more closely to the realm or kingdom of God. The preacher, thus understood, seeks to empower the congregation through education, providing critical pedagogical tools and alternative ways of seeing the world that conform to biblical perspectives. Without invoking a theology of preaching in which God is the primary actor or speaker, Voelz argues that sermons must move to hope and challenge the "dis-imagining machine" of contemporary societies. Preachers reading Voelz will be inspired to foster within their congregations critical minds and acts dedicated to alleviating human suffering.

The aim of the series is to be practical, to provide concrete guidelines and exercises for preachers to follow, and to assist them in engaging practices. Preaching is much more than art, yet by ensuring that we as preachers employ artistry in our preaching, we assist the Holy Spirit in communicating the gospel to a new generation of people seeking God.

—Paul Scott Wilson, Series Editor

Acknowledgments

The seeds of this book are found within my doctoral dissertation turned book, *Youthful Preaching* (Cascade, 2015) where I engaged the work of Henry Giroux to think about representations of adolescent youth in the literature of preaching. So I cannot begin this book without acknowledging again the community that nurtured that project into existence: the Homiletics and Liturgics Department at Vanderbilt Divinity School. Thanks to my professors and student colleagues who continue to affirm the importance of our collective work.

Since that book, I concluded a pastoral ministry with a wonderful congregation, the Johns Creek Christian Church (Disciples of Christ). There I began working with the ideas of this book more fully both in the pulpit and on paper. This congregation was supportive of my academic work as a dimension of my pastoral identity, and when the time came, they graciously commissioned me and my family to the next phase of our journey.

That next phase has been as a member of the faculty of Union Presbyterian Seminary in Richmond, Virginia, where I began serving as Assistant Professor of Preaching and Worship in 2016. I am grateful to serve among this community committed to being "the church in the world." President Brian Blount (who has provided a sermon for the book), Academic Dean Ken Mc-Fayden, the Practical Theology–Christian Education Department, other colleagues, and students have been incredibly supportive in my early work here.

Four important people passed from this life as this book took shape. The summer after my first year on faculty at Union, my father, David D. Voelz Sr. passed away suddenly and unexpectedly at the age of sixty-seven. While he was not a pastor, he and my mother nurtured my love of the church. He was my number one supporter in all dimensions of my life and I regret that, among a host of other things, he will not see this book come to life. He never missed an opportunity to tell me that he loved me and that he was proud of me. This book is dedicated to his memory and faithful witness.

Not too many weeks preceding my father's death, longtime professor of preaching and worship at Vanderbilt Divinity School, David G. Buttrick passed away. I only had Professor Buttrick for one course during my first year at Vanderbilt, so I will not pretend that I knew him well. Nonetheless, his work has been influential on me, especially in his dogged dedication to preaching the *basileia tou Theou*. I am certain readers will see this influence in the pages of this book.

Third, as I began writing in earnest, Professor Dale P. Andrews passed away from a short battle with cancer. Dale came to Vanderbilt in my final year as a student. I served as a TA for his Introduction to Preaching Class and he became the fourth reader on my dissertation committee. His thoughtfulness, challenge, genuine interest, and exuberant energy made the final push to graduation enjoyable. Our guild will miss his insight, his prophetic spirit, his presence, his warm embrace, and his unmistakable laugh.

Fourth, not long after I sent off the initial draft of this book to the publisher, our seminary community suffered the stinging loss of our beloved colleague and trailblazing scholar of womanist theological ethics, Katie Geneva Cannon. I grieve that I did not have the opportunity to know Dr. Cannon as well as I would have liked, but she was on the search committee that brought me to Union and quickly became a fiery supporter. Dr. Cannon and I had a running joke about her good but unfulfilled intentions to buy me lunch; I look forward to the day we feast together in the fullness of God's realm.

Many individuals have been more directly influential in this project. Jake Myers initially asked me to submit an essay for the journal *Practical Matters*, in which I first explored these ideas. The Justice and Ethics working group of the Academy of Homiletics read a paper that provided helpful comment for further development. Sam Persons Parkes, Lead D. Schade, Phil Snider, and Union Presbyterian Seminary student Marcy Wright provided immeasurably helpful comments on an early draft of the book. Students Heather Woodworth Brannon, Linda Fox, Gary Hatter, Mike Jaworski, Emily Nyce, Sam Shields, and Marcy Wright engaged a draft of the book in my Fall 2018 course "Proclaiming Justice in the Church and Public Square." All of these colleagues have made this book better. My thanks to the Abingdon Press staff that gave their time and energy into helping this project come to life: Connie Stella and Laurie Vaughen.

Finally, the support and encouragement of my spouse, Meredith, and daughter, Elly, have been immeasurable. I have watched over Meredith's shoulder through her career as a transformational educator and she has been this preacher's teacher on numerous occasions.

Preface

I sometimes worry that the nomenclature of "prophetic preaching" has worn thin in our current context. Not the idea of it and certainly not the practice of prophetic preaching, nor even the very fine works that have emerged to describe it, but rather labeling what we (might) do as prophetic preaching. Even if this kind of preaching mentality doesn't raise the ire of listeners, it may still put them in a defensive stance, if it means anything at all to them. Nowadays, a growing number of clergy seem to be posturing themselves as prophetic preachers. It seems that our times demand it. For those who have served in pastoral ministry for any length, we know that "the prophet" is a weighty mantle to bear. But there are so many other demands for preaching. We preach to bring healing and provide care; we preach to inspire faithful giving; we preach to allow the Bible to be heard and known in an increasingly biblically illiterate church; we preach for repentance; we preach to call others into relationship with God; and we preach to imagine other ways of being and relating to one another.

As a pastor, I worried about the moments in which I felt I needed to "perform" as a prophetic preacher. Now, to be clear, I had no problem speaking truthfully about pressing issues that I thought faith communities needed to see through the lens of faith—even issues where my silence might have been preferred. And believe me, there were those who made that abundantly clear to me! But this decision to put on the prophetic hat for a moment seemed false to me. I felt as if I was juggling my pastoral identity from one week to the next where one hat felt a lot heavier than another. And perhaps it seemed that way to my people too. So I began to wonder if there might be another way to frame how I saw my week-to-week moments in the pulpit.

I come from the Christian Church (Disciples of Christ), which is an heir to the wider Reformed tradition. One of the early leaders of this tradition, Alexander Campbell, used "teaching" to describe what we commonly call preaching. I also teach in a seminary associated with the Presbyterian Church (USA), which of course claims John Calvin as one of its historical forebears. As we will see, Calvin preferred the term *teacher* as well. The idea of the preacher-as-teacher has deep historical roots. And even now many of us can point to the resurgence of this title in many congregations, especially those with multi-staff situations, that use the term *teaching pastor* to talk about the role of the one tasked with preaching on a weekly basis.

Only after I encountered the field of critical pedagogy in the works of Paulo Freire, Henry Giroux, bell hooks, Peter McLaren, and others, did I see potential to reframe what we do as preaching to teach. In these educators, I came to see a body of literature questioning the foundational premises of teaching as currently practiced in the US context, calling teachers to think about teaching as enacting radical democratic practice in the search to alleviate oppression and domination. In the ways that they talked about the practices of education and the work of teachers, I saw deep similarities with what I hope preaching does. So I began to wonder if the idea of the preacher-as-teacher might be critically reappropriated in a time of deep cultural division, strife, and weariness.

What you will find in these pages is just that: a project to find a more holistic image of preaching so that preachers can avoid the frantic juggling we do among the many other tasks of preaching each week, especially in these divided times, not to mention all the other tasks of ministry with which we are charged. Except in brief, I do not put forward traditional understandings of the preacher-as-teacher. I do not propose ten new ways to help your congregation learn the stories or themes of the Bible. Instead, I seek to outline ways that the image of the teacher might help us see our preaching not as a constellation of many different images and tasks, but perhaps a way to fit it all under one roof. I introduce the field of critical pedagogy as a conversation partner not for redefining the tasks of preaching for our time, but rather to rename them in more appropriate ways, especially the ones we've called "prophetic," almost by default. Hopefully you will see resonances with what you are already doing, even as I introduce new concepts and frames for preaching. In the resonances with your own preaching, I hope you will feel affirmed, even as I hope to push us all to speak boldly about important issues as our country continues to cascade toward polarization and our own echo chambers.

I hope that in reading this book you will not only see your ministry of preaching differently, but that together with God we might work toward the transformation of this world into what God is calling it to be.

Introduction
Chalk Talk

Images of Preaching and the Preacher-as-Teacher

On the morning of Wednesday, July 22, 2015, not more than two miles from the insulated, exurban congregation outside Atlanta, Georgia, where I was serving as a pastor, a man used a gun to take the lives of his wife, their two children, his wife's father, and eventually, his own. I happened to be in Columbus, Ohio, for the General Assembly of the Christian Church (Disciples of Christ), which is the biennial gathering of my tradition. That same day, after some contentious discussion, the assembly adopted a resolution concerning gun violence (GA-1521).[1] The resolution calls on the church to examine the role of guns in our communities and to work with faith communities as well as community partners to reduce the pervasiveness of gun violence.

Emboldened by the concurrence of these two events, I resolved to preach on gun violence on the coming Sunday, as I had on other crisis events that occurred over the span of my ministry. I knew this was a topic upon which the congregation would likely be divided and where my silence might be preferred. Honestly, in terms of the construction of the sermon, it was not my best. The week was shortened by our gathering, and while the work with the biblical text and the events at hand were faithful, the sermon's construction was messy. However, I employed my tradition's call to individual interpretation and covenant in community, and I did so in a reasonable and compelling way. I called us to reflection and vigilance about our individual and collective participation in gun culture. Reactions to the sermon were mixed, with extremes on either side in the moments and days to follow. A few took it upon themselves to inform me that it would be better if I were indeed silent on this topic primarily because of how they understood the separation of church and state. I received a multipage letter from one person and a forty-minute monologue phone call from another, who eventually took their membership and their tithe elsewhere. In their minds preaching should not interfere in the social and political issues of the day. I had gone a step too far.

I share this not because my experience was unique or because I did anything special. This scenario plays out in thousands of different ways in communities of faith across the country. The topics change: mass shootings and other forms of violence, race, ethnicity, multireligious contexts, immigration, poverty, climate change, domestic and foreign terrorism, domestic and child abuse, politics, and of course, bickering about it all on social media. But as much as the topics change, the tension remains in unsettled congregations. Preachers wonder, "What can be spoken? Can I talk about *this*?" I began my life in congregational ministry only a few months prior to 9/11. And it seems that crisis preaching has been part of my time ever since, where those crises have included events surrounding weather, climate, culture, politics, or the fusion of all of these. We seem to be in constant crisis! Add to that the climate of relationships we have cultivated (or not cultivated, perhaps) since the advent of social media. We live in a weary world of division. What does the preacher say? What can the preacher say?

The many instances of crisis preaching that preachers have been called to address over the years elicit a question that precedes the laundry list of would-be taboo topics we sense being called to address or avoid in our preaching. In other words, before we can open our mouths about contentious topics in a weary, divided world, preachers must ask another question: "Who am I?" By what image of the preacher do we appropriately talk taboos and offer a word in a weary world? By what image do preachers understand their role, and as a result, how do they claim and receive authority? In this book I propose a reconsideration of an ancient image, the image of the preacher-as-teacher, modified through the contemporary lens of critical pedagogy, as a fitting image of preaching for these times.

Images of the Preacher in Recent Times

These preliminary questions of preaching identity are not new. Examining fundamental assumptions about preaching by proposing various images has almost become commonplace. These images are functional metaphors for preaching, each with a host of entailments, or implications.[2] Images of preaching often take the form of statements that begin "the preacher as" one thing or another. In doing so, preachers find a way to explore systems of beliefs about preaching, including the preacher's role and sense of authority, the work of God in preaching, the role of listeners, approach to the Bible and other sacred texts, relationship with tradition(s), understandings of the human situation, and much more.

A number of these images are explored in Thomas Long's introductory preaching textbook *The Witness of Preaching*, first published in 1989.[3] Long sketches the images of the preacher as "herald," "pastor," "storyteller/poet," and "witness" as organizing metaphors for preaching ministry. Jana Childers, leaning into a passage from John Calvin and feminist understandings, conceives of preachers as "birthing the sermon."[4] Alyce McKenzie has extended her description of the preacher as "sage" throughout her writing.[5] More recently a number of other images have come forth. The 2010 book *Slow of Speech and Unclean Lips* gathered a number of preaching scholars who proposed contemporary understandings of preaching identity through images such as: "messenger of hope," "lover," "God's mystery steward," "ridiculous person," "fisher," "host and guest," "one 'out of your mind,'" and "one entrusted."[6] Kenyatta Gilbert links the traditional images of "prophet," "priest," and "sage" into a *trivocal* image of preaching to serve preachers in African American traditions.[7] Ronald J. Allen and O. Wesley Allen have recently highlighted the idea of preaching as "conversation," and the preacher as a partner in that conversation.[8] These images help describe theologies of preaching useful for framing one's own concept of preaching rooted in critical understandings of the Bible, theology, tradition, pastoral authority, and context. So this kind of reflection is well-worn ground in recent times and, maybe, with the many options before us, combined with the times in which we live, the available lenses for imagining our work might overwhelm us.

But as helpful as each of these images are, one image of preaching has endured since early Christianity, making appearances here and there to define the necessary function(s) of preaching for the ages in which the church finds itself. This image may function more like the dependable old friend than the flashy new sidekick, but it has been trustworthy to describe the work of preaching through the centuries. In what follows, I trace the preacher-as-teacher as a kind of play in two acts, demonstrating how the preacher-as-teacher has functioned as a response to different needs through the years.

The Preacher-as-Teacher in Three Acts

Act One: Instructing the Faithful

The image of the preacher-as-teacher has significant historical roots. Drawing upon his rhetorical training, Augustine cites Cicero in what is commonly referred to as the first preaching textbook, *De Doctrina Christiana (On Christian Doctrine)*.[9] For Augustine, the Christian speaker operates with three interrelated purposes: to teach, delight, and persuade. And with regard to the nature of preaching-as-teaching, Augustine says that "true eloquence consists, not in making people like what they disliked, nor in making them do what they shrank from, but in making clear what was obscure."[10] The preacher seeks to impart knowledge or content with clarity of understanding.

In twelfth-century France, theologian Alan of Lille coined what might possibly be "the first formal definition of preaching," saying that "Preaching is an open and public instruction in faith and behavior, whose purpose is the forming of [persons]; it derives from the path of reason and from the fountainhead of the 'authorities.'"[11] The emphasis here is on instruction, meaning the preacher provides ideas and information that result in the formation of believers, with that instruction firmly grounded in the authorities of Bible, reason, and church tradition.

Many years later, John Calvin imagined *preaching-as-teaching*, and uses these two words interchangeably in the *Institutes of the Christian Religion*. Calvin observes that "although God's power is not bound to outward means, [God] has nonetheless bound us to this ordinary manner of teaching."[12] And though apostles, prophets, and evangelists are temporary offices of ministry, those who teach are those "whom the church can never go without." For Calvin, preaching-as-teaching endures as a permanent ministry. Calvin goes on to detail how teachers are charged with "scriptural interpretation—to keep doctrine whole and pure among believers."[13] This entails interpretation and explanation of the scriptures in order to preserve and further the witness of the church. Indeed, such an understanding of the preaching office continues into today as ordained ministers in the PC(USA) are designated "teaching elder," a newer development over the previous designation of "minister of word and sacrament."

In the first half of the nineteenth century, Alexander Campbell, who was one of the forebears of the Christian Church (Disciples of Christ) and an heir of the Reformed tradition, also blurred the lines between preaching and teaching. Campbell's context was the rapidly populating frontier of the Second Great Awakening, when many new converts were being swept into the fold of the church. In deference to his understanding of the scriptures, and the fact that the word *preaching* never occurs in or to the church in the New Testament, Campbell believed "that the function of preaching was never held to be a part of the program within the local church. The bishop, or pastor, was a teacher and not preacher. His (*sic*) work was edification and not conversion."[14] What we have here are two different tasks. Preaching preceded conversion and thus occurred outside the local church as evangelists witnessed to the gospel to non-Christians. Teaching, on the other hand, happened when the faithful gathered for worship, and the bishop pointed to "the meaning of his precepts, and the duties incumbent on those converted to him as the Lord Messiah."[15] Indeed Campbell much preferred the terms *lecture* over *sermon*, and *bishop*, *elder* or *pastor* over *preacher*, but this seems to be largely out of a committed (and somewhat polemical) differentiation over the roles of located clergy and evangelists.

Out of similar commitments to the biblical text around one hundred years later, New Testament scholar C. H. Dodd's book *The Apostolic Preaching and Its Development* set the stage for studied consideration of the function of preaching in the early twentieth century.[16] In that work, Dodd famously makes the distinction between *kerygma* and *didache*, (preaching and teaching) based on close examination of the New Testament. For Dodd,

> There is a clear distinction between preaching and teaching, and this can be found in the Gospels, Acts, Epistles, and Apocalypse. Teaching is ethical instruction in most instances, though in particular instances it might be called apologetic, "the reasoned commendation of Christianity to persons interested but not yet convinced." Preaching is the public proclamation of Christianity to the non-Christian world.[17]

Dodd was able to make this distinction, he believed, by distilling a specific formulaic content for Christian *kerygma* throughout the New Testament. Teaching and preaching were a result of different content for different occasions. While highly influential at the time, this distinction has not withstood the test of time. The sharp separation between preaching and teaching as wholly different in content and occasion, at least as outlined by Dodd, has blurred.[18]

Throughout the early church context, the late Middle Ages, the Reformation, and the growing North American church context, Christian preaching has been classified as teaching for a blossoming, growing church that needed instruction for a growing faith. Or, as for Campbell and Dodd, teaching served as a functional way to distinguish the church's internal oral communication from the type of evangelistic proclamation that happened to bring others into the fold of the church. As the curtain closed on this kind of distinction, another appeared.

Act Two: Reaction to Changes in North American Christianity

Act Two of the preacher-as-teacher responds to the shifts in the context of North American Christianity and the homiletical turn to the needs of the listener. In the early- to mid-1990s, the image of the preacher-as-teacher made a resurgence. In response to mainline denominational decline and a rise in congregants who knew less about their faith in terms of biblical and doctrinal knowledge, Ronald Allen and Clark Williamson wrote *The Teaching Minister* in 1991 and Allen *The Teaching Sermon* in 1995.[19] In *The Teaching Minister*, Williamson and Allen declare:

> Preaching itself, for example, is seldom an evangelistic proclamation to a crowd of people who have never before heard of the Christian faith. Usually it is a presentation to a congregation of Christian people who, whatever their understandings of things Christ, have at least taken the risk of exposing themselves to the gospel. While every sermon should no doubt announce the good news to these people, it should also, and for the greater part, be at pains to teach it to them, to help them come to understanding it and their lives in relationship to each other.[20]

While this sounds much like Campbell and Dodd, the situation differs because it is one of decline rather than growth. Allen goes on to lament how the church is in a "theological malaise" and congregants are increasingly "theologically illiterate."[21] The impulse to preaching-as-teaching comes as an adjustment to the situation of listeners, not as a fundamental starting place.

Thomas Long raises the issue of teaching as well, though in somewhat different tones. As Long raises criticism on North American preaching's focus on experience through narrative preaching, he returns to Augustine and the dictum that preaching teaches, delights, and persuades. But instead of making a statement about individual sermons, Long refers rather to "seasons in the history of preaching. There are cultural moments that require the inflection to slant this way or that. There are times when the pulpit needs to become a lectern, and the emphasis falls on teaching the people."[22] And for Long, the pendulum has swung too far in the direction of delight. People of mainstream Christianity through the latter middle of the twentieth century were knowledgeable about the Christian faith. But they were disenchanted and preachers responded with story-formed preaching and other revolutions in sermon form. Now the opposite situation exists. A return to teaching is in order so that listeners might faithfully know and, therefore, faithfully interpret with their own lives the living Christian tradition.

Alyce McKenzie identifies a similar kind of imbalance as Long, noting "the divide between teaching and delighting in our preaching, because preaching today is living a double life with a double identity: teaching or entertainment."[23] On the one hand, she indicates the "six points and a PowerPoint" school of preaching, which assumes that listeners do not know basics of the faith. By this, McKenzie means that teaching sermons are propositional, deductive/linear, and as a result, often quite boring. To illustrate the importance of preaching that teaches, we might notice the surge in ministry staffs who employ someone with the title of "teaching pastor," denoting the person that leads the movement in worship we might ordinarily call "Ministry of the Word."[24] On the other side of the double life lies the "experience" school that employs stories and images to help foster connections with listeners' emotions and experiences, rather than the limited prospect of the intellect. Like Long following Augustine, we might call this "delight" or as McKenzie does somewhat disparagingly, "entertainment." The problem is that the divide between sermons that rely on reason and those that rely on imagination has become a great chasm. And what McKenzie envisions are sermons that close that gap: sermons that teach with imagination. She advocates for preaching that "activate[s] the power of the imagination to teach the mind and engage the emotions and the will. The more people need basic teaching, the more our sermons need for it to be presented in imaginative ways."[25] But the fact remains: preaching-as-teaching is about content.

Robert Reid believes that teaching is one among four voices the preacher assumes, where the "teaching voice...call[s] forth faith" and "the sermon is one that invites listeners to affirm the ideas presented as representative of a confessional or an interpretive tradition."[26] Again, teaching becomes an exercise in presenting content to be consumed by the congregation and digested with either affirmation or disagreement.

Paul Scott Wilson comes to a different conclusion about the relationship between preaching and teaching, ultimately determining that rather than too little teaching, there has been a significant amount of teaching, but its scope has been too limited in the overall task of preaching. He first provides a helpful definition as to the nature of teaching: "Teaching provides the theological, historical, and cultural information that listeners need to understand who God is, has been, and will be; it explores the thought of our forebears and leads to new understandings appropriate for the present; and it guides life and prayer."[27] This is not unlike what we have seen before in this brief survey: teaching provides *information* that assists understanding about God, interacts with the resources of tradition, and guides into faith formation. But whereas others believe there has not been enough of this to support the church, Wilson believes that there has not been enough of the kind of preaching-teaching that "is also about molding character and helping people better to live the lives that Christ calls disciples to live."[28]

Deepening his criticism, Wilson goes on to differentiate further between teaching and proclamation. While proclamation assumes that teaching happens in sermons, proclamation reaches beyond teaching in that it is not simply "about" the gospel but rather performs the gospel, "offer[ing] God in substantial ways in the sermon, to speak on God's behalf wonderful words of reconciling love, to facilitate a meeting between God and hearers in light of the cross, to make space for Christ in the Holy Spirit to encounter hearers from beyond the grave...Where teaching leaves the load of responsibility on the hearer to do something, proclamation removes it, or rather Christ does, in and through proclamation."[29] Wilson's point is more than technical and functional (as with Dodd's distinction between *kerygma* and *didache* or Campbell's differentiation in audience). Proclamation is theological and christological, reaching into some of the deepest questions of homiletical theology: How is it that God/Christ/Spirit are present in preaching and how do they function in the relation between preacher and listener? Wilson believes that this is something that preaching-as-teaching cannot access. For Wilson, preaching is limited and settles for less than its worth when it functions merely as theological teaching; however, in proclamation, hearers and preacher alike are directly addressed *by* God through an eventful encounter *with* God.

So where does this leave us? It seems that in Act Two, teaching is a necessary *function* of preaching, and it accomplishes that function by the ongoing instruction, catechesis, formation, and edification of the faithful (or would-be faithful) who are no longer as informed as they were in days gone by. In both the mainline denominational and evangelical or nondenominational contexts, teaching seems to be in short supply to meet the biblical and theological illiteracy of the day. And as a corollary, teaching operates (or at least it can) as a particular rhetorical style of preaching. In other words, teaching happens in preaching through content choices, sermon designs, and delivery. Or, for someone who takes Wilson's approach, too much teaching has cost the church a more significant kind of preaching (proclamation). In teaching *about* God, preachers have left listeners without an encounter *with* God. In the debate between rhetoric and theology, rhetoric seems to have won the day according to Wilson.[30] Again, teaching operates as a function of preaching, but for Wilson does not achieve its greater purposes. The problem becomes that these descriptions of preaching-as-teaching render a flat, one-dimensional concept of preaching-as-teaching. Teaching becomes limited to certain functions or a limited theological life. And as a result, as Tom Long notes, the image of the preacher-as-teacher only makes appearances when it might be needed. When the pendulum swings again, what happens to the preacher-as-teacher? Contrary to Calvin's sense of the permanency of this office, while we might call preachers teachers, Long might say that the designation depends on the seasonal needs of the church's context. Moreover, we get little sense of how preaching-as-teaching intervenes to provide a word to sustain a weary world or does more than provide content for the theologically uninformed and unformed listener. A third act to the preacher-as-teacher is in order.

When joined with more contemporary thinking around what is commonly called "critical pedagogy," the image can be more expansive, more comprehensive, and especially suitable for meeting the needs of a weary world. In recasting this image, the preacher does not have to choose between teacher one Sunday and prophet the next, or vacillate between the four voices outlined by Robert Reid, or ping-pong between any other images for that matter. It does not serve to replace the functions of preaching-as-teaching I have described above. Nor does it add a new image to the catalog that has come to our attention in recent years. Rather, through critical pedagogy we discover additional dimensions to the tasks of the preacher-as-teacher, augmenting those that have been expressed since Augustine's dictum. As a result, the preacher-as-teacher can undergird all aspects of preaching. Rather than relegating teaching to a silo of preaching waiting to be brought out from time to time, the time has come to reimagine how we think of preaching-as-teaching to be more comprehensive. Such additions also serve to avoid the possible fragmentation of preaching identity we might see or feel as preachers who feel pressure to accomplish so many different tasks among our listeners. And it avoids the temptation to imagine preaching-as-teaching as a kind of simple pedantic didacticism or what Allen calls the preacher as the conversational "cafeteria manager

who passes options before the learners."[31] The chapters of this book make
this case and offer a fuller definition of preaching-as-teaching that can help
meet the challenges of weary and divided listeners in a fragmented world.
But first, we need to introduce a partner who can help carry us into this
third act.

Act Three: Critical Pedagogy as a Partner for Preaching

Critical pedagogy questions the exercise of power and domination in
teaching practices, working toward teaching that promotes the agency of
individuals and the pursuit of social justice for society as a whole. Two major foundations have been laid in the history of critical pedagogy. First,
and perhaps most famously, is the work of Brazilian educator Paulo Freire,
who in his 1970 *Pedagogy of the Oppressed* famously criticized "banking"
methods of education wherein the powerful transmit learning to the often-
illiterate masses, the content and delivery of which serves the interest of
oppressive regimes.[32] Freire imagines methods of teaching that raise the
critical consciousness of students as they learn to read and write, a process
he called "conscientization." In this view, education becomes not simply a
set of skills acquired for uncritical reproduction of cultural values (as defined by the powerful elite), but a practice of freedom and liberation for
oppressed peoples.

The second intellectual foundation is commonly known as the Frankfurt School, which emerges in the work of Freire's intellectual heirs. Of
these, Henry Giroux has been the most prolific of writers, and even though
his work has expanded to cultural studies, politics, popular culture, and
critical youth studies, his earlier work in critical pedagogy will serve as the
major conversation partner for most of this book. But others, who draw
the conversation into the North American context, include Joe Kincheloe,
bell hooks, Peter McLaren, and others. Along with Freire's influence, Giroux leans heavily on Frankfurt School social theorists Theodor W. Adorno,
Max Horkheimer, and Herbert Marcuse. Unlike Freire, these thinkers did
not work in the areas of teaching and learning but composed a group of
scholars in the early twentieth century interested in the historical, cultural,
economic, and political production of knowledge and power (not simply
economic, as with Karl Marx). The range of theoretical influences beyond
the Frankfurt School is immense, but not indiscriminate, always seeking
theories that through various disciplinary partners account for and then
work to alleviate human suffering.[33]

While Freire's focus was on education practices in the context of op-pression in South America, Giroux and other adherents of critical pedagogy in North America attend to teaching and learning that leads toward human flourishing and participatory democracy at all educational levels. For the North American context, this results in a definition of critical pedagogy convinced that:

> Pedagogy is not a method but a moral and political practice, one that rec-ognizes the relationship between knowledge and power, and at the same time realizes that central to all pedagogical practices is a struggle over agency, power, politics, and the formative cultures that make a radical democracy possible. This view of pedagogy does not mould, but inspires, and at the same time it is directive, capable of imagining a better world, the unfinished nature of agency, and the need to consistently reimagine a democracy that is never finished. In this sense, critical pedagogy is a form of educated hope committed to producing young people capable and willing to expand and deepen their sense of themselves, to think the "world" critically, "to imagine something other than their own well-being," to serve the public good, take risks, and struggle for a substantive democracy that is now in a state of acute crisis as the dark clouds of totalitarianism are increasingly threatening to destroy democracy itself on a global scale.[34]

This entails more than simply supplying content and information. And as we will see, this supplies some critical frames through which we might see the practice of preaching.

In the next four chapters I will draw out some of the features of critical pedagogy that make this a helpful new partner to integrate into our existing image of the preacher-as-teacher. As stated above, these implications revise and expand earlier notions of the preacher-as-teacher so that it might func-tion more holistically and comprehensively, rather than on an as-needed basis. And I believe the image can bridge the rhetoric-theology debate; I make the case that preaching-as-teaching also performs a major theological task (which Wilson demurs, in favor of the term *proclamation*).

Chapter 1 explores the preacher as a public and transformational intel-lectual, someone who contributes to the formation of public life beyond the walls of the church. Chapter 2 assesses critical pedagogy's insistence that teachers teach toward a vision of the public sphere, and how this is incum-bent upon the preacher as well. Chapter 3 outlines the vision of the kinds of teaching practices used in critical pedagogy, which lead to both critique and possibility/hope and how they intersect with preaching. Chapter 4 analyzes the relationship between the preacher-as-teacher, the congregation, and notions of authority, and thus the "teaching sermon" itself. As with learning a new partner for preaching, we will need to learn some new vocabulary and concepts. I hope to introduce these in ways that are not laborious for those not familiar with the literature of critical pedagogy. Chapter 5 will turn to describing some possible sermon forms and three sermon examples that display qualities of the preacher-as-teacher.

Chapter One

Beyond Information

The Preacher as Transformational Intellectual

> *...I celebrate teaching that enables transgressions—a movement against and beyond boundaries. It is that movement which makes education the practice of freedom.*[1]
> —bell hooks

I suspect that it might be more than a bit off-putting when I propose we think about preachers as intellectuals. Doesn't that sound high-brow and elitist? As congregants talk with each other about their pastors, who wants their reputation to be, "Well, our pastor is such an intellectual!"? As Tom Long recognizes about the recent history of preaching, "Indeed, not so very long ago it was held that the primary problem of most preaching was that it was pedantic. While the world was coming apart at the seams, preachers were holding class, fogging up sanctuaries, churning out 'teachy' sermons, paraphrasing Kittel's Theological Wordbook, tediously connecting the hipbone of justification to the thighbone of sanctification."[2] Long is right. At first glance, the idea that preachers are intellectuals might make us conjure images of dull, lifeless, and disconnected preaching. The idea of the preacher-as-teacher in this mode should make us shudder.

Long goes on to identify a parallel problem with sermon listeners: "The problem...is that it is more and more evident that the preacher stands before a congregation that does not know the content of the Christian faith....Moreover, it is not only biblical awareness that has been damaged, but also the capacity to employ theological language."[3] Long identifies the challenge as the inability of Christians to see their faith as a "comprehensive way of seeing and being in the world."⁴

But there is more at stake here. Preaching-as-teaching goes beyond helping congregations use the knowledge they glean from the pulpit as an interpretive framework for life. Critical pedagogy helps reframe the function of teaching such that the preacher-as-teacher becomes more than someone who simply helps his or her listeners "know something" so that knowledge can be used in a kind of instrumental way. In what follows, we will trace the contours of how the preacher-as-teacher functions as a *transformational* intellectual through the lens of critical pedagogy. This dimension of the preacher-as-teacher functions not just as a different nomenclature; rather it initiates us into a different way of inhabiting the role of teacher.

Thinking Differently about Teaching

What do teachers do? What is their purpose? The answer to this question is hotly contested. The old answer to the question is the "Three R's: Reading, Writing, and Arithmetic." In this cultural idiom, teachers give students skills to accomplish basic functions. A newer answer, not too distantly related, surrounds standardized testing. Student achievement and teacher success depend on how well students can meet established criteria measured by standardized tests. But to what end? Though there are some impulses in conversations around public education to think about student success beyond the numbers, measures of teacher and student success continue to lie in grades, test scores, and grade point averages. But might there be something more to teaching than simply a transfer of knowledge or content? Or more than helping prepare students to enter the workforce?

The answers to those questions lie at the heart of those who work in critical pedagogy. The flashpoint for thinking more critically about the ends of education, and the teacher-student relationship was Brazilian educator Paulo Freire's groundbreaking, influential *Pedagogy of the Oppressed*, first published in 1970. Perhaps most famous to Freire's work is the idea of the "banking concept of education," which he described as a process in which "the teacher issues communiqués and makes deposits which the students patiently receive, memorize, and repeat.... The scope of action allowed to the students extends only as far as receiving, filing, and storing the deposits."⁵ We can easily visualize the practices associated with this: students seated quietly in rows, copying notes from a board, or filling out worksheets, while the communication remains mostly one-directional from teacher to student. Freire posits that this type of education functions as a mirror of an oppressive society in the following ways:

a) the teacher teaches and the students are taught;
b) the teacher knows everything and the students know nothing;
c) the teacher thinks and the students are thought about;
d) the teacher talks and the students listen—meekly;
e) the teacher disciplines and the students are disciplined;
f) the teacher chooses and enforces his (*sic*) choice, and the students comply;
g) the teacher acts and the students have the illusion of acting through the action of the teacher;
h) the teacher chooses the program content, and the students (who were not consulted) adapt to it;
i) the teacher confuses the authority of knowledge with his or her own professional authority, which she and he sets in opposition to the freedom of the students;
j) the teacher is the Subject of the learning process, while the pupils are mere objects.[6]

Freire's critique of this process is that students simply become managers of content: their success depends on their capacity to memorize and rehearse that which they learn. And as such, students do not develop the types of critical consciousness necessary to intervene in and transform the world around them, which is just as oppressors would have it.[7] As an example of this, elsewhere Freire cites some samples of the kind of simplistic reading texts used in adult literacy campaigns used in developing countries. To name just one example Freire gives, one such text reads: "If you hammer a nail, be careful not to smash your finger."[8] Freire contends that this kind of text in no way helps working-class and oppressed adults just learning to read imagine a way out of their situation. And in addition, this practice reinscribes power dynamics at work in society.

This supplies just a brief orientation to Freire's critique of teaching, and the beginning of Freire's impulse to make teaching a practice of freedom, "critical intervention," and liberation, rather than a practice that reinforces domination.[9] When shifted to the North American context, however, we see a different context: autocratic, totalitarian governments do not conduct the kinds of systematic oppression and violence that characterized Freire's Latin American setting. In this context, adherents of critical pedagogy recalibrate the principles and practices Freire outlined. Among those adherents, Henry Giroux has been among the most prolific in terms of writing production. As teacher authority (speaking of their ability to self-determine teaching content and practices) has diminished in the North American educational landscape, Giroux often calls teachers "public intellectuals" or "transformative intellectuals." As I pointed out above, use of "intellectual" might come as a jarring, odd, or perhaps even elitist way to describe a teacher. Who would imagine designating their child's kindergarten teacher, for instance, as a transformational intellectual? Giroux senses the dissonance and explains it with three reasons. First, this terminology helps describe the work of a teacher as a kind of "intellectual labor" rather than thinking of teachers and their work "in purely instrumental or technical terms." In other words, something different is afoot here than humans who employ a kind of prescribed set of skills or practices to achieve a uniform end. Teachers are not involved in the formulaic, predictable production of a product. Education is not an assembly line. Second, this terminology helps provide some ground for the "kinds of ideological and practical conditions necessary for teachers to function as intellectuals." Giroux believes teachers are deeply involved in work that needs space for reflection and theory. Third, the terminology helps provide clarity around "the role that teachers play in producing and legitimating various political, economic and social interests" that come to bear through various pedagogical practices.[10] Giroux's description of the teacher as transformative intellectual has at least three important corollaries that describe the role and work of the teacher.

First, teachers are *reflective practitioners*. As an intellectual activity, teaching is a practice that is consistently refined by considering new realities, changing conditions, and multiple constituencies. Despite teacher education and training that center around efficient teaching and classroom management, teaching can never be reduced to "applied science."[11] Teachers bring educational theory as well as political and social theory to bear when thinking through curriculum and in the classroom, "integrating thinking and practice," which undergoes constant revision in the ongoing loop between theory and practice.[12] No false separations, mono-directional pathways, or hierarchy exist between theory and practice. In fact, theory can be conceived as a liberating practice, as educator bell hooks discerns.[13]

Second, teachers teach with the goal of empowering others to engage in critical thinking. Being a reflective practitioner is never self-serving, nor is it measured in bureaucratized educational assessments. Teachers aim not to improve standardized test scores as if that is some end, but rather "to teach students to think critically, to learn how to affirm their own experiences, and to understand the need to struggle individually and collectively for a more just society."[14] This means that students do not simply digest content. They actively engage in thinking about how their learning intersects with their personal and social contexts. They question whose histories and literature are present in the curriculum and why. For critical pedagogy, learning and being are thoroughly intertwined.[15] So learning which fosters critical thinking integrally relates to how teachers and learners exist in the world.

Third, and related, teachers do not teach toward tacit reproduction of the cultural status quo, but rather toward transformation. Critical pedagogy recognizes that schools are implicitly sites of political and cultural struggle. Schools are "economic, cultural, and social sites that are inextricably linked to the issues of power and control. This means that schools do more than pass on in an objective fashion on a common set of values and knowledge.... As such, schools serve to introduce and legitimate particular forms of social life."[16] Again and again, Giroux refers to schools as "contested spheres," meaning that there is struggle about the kinds of knowledge and values to which students are exposed. We see this in arguments over what counts as valid history and science, which books are allowed, and what approach schools take toward religion. So when Giroux and others see teachers as transformative intellectuals, they see teachers as people who "make knowledge problematic; utilize critical and affirming dialogue; and make the case for struggling for a qualitatively better world for all people."[17]

By employing these terms, Giroux advocates for teachers as pivotal contributors to the formation of public life. An understanding of teaching as a public, transformative, and intellectual activity results in a form of cultural politics, helping students "develop a social imagination and civic courage capable of helping them to intervene in their own self-formation, in the formation of others, and in the socially reproductive cycle of life in general."[18] I will say more about these related matters in subsequent chapters.

One final note before transitioning to how we might consider the preacher through critical pedagogy. Giroux and others point to teaching as a practice that provides regular interventions in the lives of students. For Giroux, "education is a form of political intervention in the world and is capable of creating the possibilities for social transformation.... Rather than viewing teaching as technical practice, radical pedagogy in the broadest terms is a moral and political practice premised on the assumption that learning is not about processing received knowledge but about actually transforming it."[19] And for bell hooks, educators teach to "transgress." For critical pedagogy, a certain quality to the practice of teaching makes it interruptive, disruptive, and transgressive, intervening into the social, political, and economic conditions of students' everyday lives for very specific liberating purposes. The transformational intellectual labors toward these ends.

Preacher as Transformational Intellectual

What does all this have to do with preaching? Yes, at times the preacher steps into the pulpit with the intent to teach in a traditional sense: the preacher dusts off an old doctrine with fresh language, interprets a difficult passage of scripture, employs the historical-critical method to give contextual background to a scripture, or even gives some perspective on a hot-button topic. This is, after all, what a recent Gallup poll tells us people are seeking. Churchgoers want sermons that (1) teach them more about scripture and (2) help them connect religion to their own lives.[20] Isn't this enough to satisfy our definition of teaching?

The problem with this, of course, is that this produces a rather flat account of the power and potential of preaching. As I write the first draft of this chapter, the tragedy in Charlottesville has occurred. As a result of white nationalism and its insidious anti-Semitism and racism, a thirty-two-year-old woman named Heather Heyer was murdered when protest and counter-protest converged. Just days before, the world looked on as a seeming nuclear standoff between the United States and North Korea unfolded. Only a week or two removed, the monumental hurricanes Harvey and Irma struck—further examples of catastrophic weather events exacerbated by climate disruption. Sandwiched between the two, the DACA program was rescinded, threatening close to a million US-born children of immigrants. Faced with these enormous challenges, merely teaching "more about scripture" in our preaching hardly seems worth the effort.

Of course, preaching can be prophetic, seeking to provoke transformation. But as I said earlier, such prophetic preaching produces anxiety among preachers who feel it necessary to muster the courage to preach prophetically *this Sunday*. Nora Tisdale rightly points to seven resistances to prophetic preaching:

1. An inherited model of biblical interpretation that marginalizes the prophetic dimensions of Scripture

2. Pastoral concern for parishioners

3. Fear of conflict

4. Fear of dividing a congregation

5. Fear of being disliked, rejected, or made to pay a price for prophetic witness

6. Feelings of inadequacy in addressing prophetic concerns

7. Discouragement that our own prophetic witness is not making a difference[21]

Tisdale goes on to note that the aversion to prophetic preaching is not wrong, and that pastors should seek "some sort of balance between the prophetic and the pastoral."[22] Despite helpfully tying together the pastoral and prophetic functions, preachers may still experience a kind of juggling act for their preaching, having to decide when one's preaching ministry has become too prophetic in the eyes of others and not pastoral enough, and vice versa. And this is no less difficult even when the prophetic sermon serves pastoral needs! In my own preaching experience, this kind of constant self-assessment was maddening and perhaps unhealthy. And I wonder just how long preachers can bear the weight of preaching prophetically in their community.

Herein lies the connection to teaching. Rather than having to assess whether our preaching was prophetic enough for our congregation (or our clergy peers!), I propose that we use a different measure, if you will. Or, really, no measure at all. I do not mean that we get to excuse ourselves from self-assessment. Instead, in a fuller account of preaching-as-teaching, preaching that we might have characterized as prophetic no longer falls on a kind of continuum between prophetic or pastoral, or some kind of blend of the two, for which Tisdale makes the case in her book. From my personal experience, this assessment of the pastoral and prophetic dynamic was entirely too anxiety-producing to maintain, especially given the dizzying pace with which catastrophic news events unfold in the digital age. Thus, I contend that preaching-as-teaching through the lens of critical pedagogy can help bear this weight, so to speak, because preaching-as-teaching encompasses more than just giving biblical and theological information to uninformed, mostly passive listeners.

Intervention

Let's start where we left off in the discussion of features of critical pedagogy's account of the transformational and public intellectual. While there are many ways to think about and articulate regular worship gatherings where preaching occurs, through critical pedagogy we might see preaching as a regular intervention into the lives of those who gather. This intervention is not simply for the gathering of information about the Bible, or even making connections to life beyond the walls of church gatherings. Knowledge about the Bible can never be the *telos*. As Harry Emerson Fosdick humorously remarked in 1928, "Only the preacher proceeds still upon the idea that folk come to church desperately anxious to discover what happened to the Jebusites."[23] Fosdick recognized that preaching-as-teaching was a limited enterprise. But his sense that preaching should simply begin with and speak to the deep concerns of the listener, commonly known as Fosdick's "project method," was a limited, therapy-centered corrective.

Instead, preaching in the midst of worship gatherings functions not unlike how Giroux describes teaching and learning as interventions: "schools actually are contested spheres that embody and express a struggle over what forms of authority, types of knowledge, forms of moral regulation and versions of the past and future should be legitimated and transmitted to students."[24] Preaching-as-teaching regularly intervenes in the lives of those who gather, recognizing that those gathered *already* recognize that our lives are "contested spheres." Those who gather for worship largely gather with this sense, despite widely different theological orientations. Life as it is (personally and communally) and life as God would have it bring people into contested spheres. The problem, of course, is that while many still attend churches anticipating some kind of regular intervention (we might think about *what kinds of intervention* weekly churchgoers seek), in many circles where we see decline in church attendance, the regular interventions of preaching and liturgy have not been so compelling as to be worthwhile when compared with other priorities and commitments. Preaching-as-teaching seeks to make plain and speak into this struggle, articulating how faith navigates these contested spheres. Chapter 2 will more fully discuss the nature of these contested spheres. For now, it is enough to point out that the preacher-as-teacher makes regular interventions into this contestation.

Critical Thinking

Rather than focusing solely on sending sermon listeners out to perform actions in the community (perhaps as much a form of authoritarianism as conveying knowledge, even from a progressive or liberal perspective), the preacher-as-teacher as public and transformational intellectual captures the thought of Marx, Horkheimer, and some political theologians that "critical thought generates transformative action."[25] The preacher-as-teacher as public or transformative intellectual uses the sermon as an exercise in critical thinking in order to help the faithful exercise their agency in and beyond the ecclesial sphere. Remember that critical pedagogy seeks to make plain how education as a cultural practice is integrated into a web of social, economic, and political relationships. So it is with each new preaching moment. This is critical thinking with the congregation. The preacher-as-teacher seeks to expose, examine, and help listeners assess the social, economic, political, and theological relationships that undergird daily life. In the words of Giroux, we might say that preaching "must do everything possible to provide students [listeners] with the knowledge and skills they need to learn how to deliberate, make judgments, and exercise choice."[26] Preaching makes regular interventions into the lives of listeners to help them think in ways that empower them for transformative living. The knowledge gained from the pulpit is not apolitical or neutral, nor does it result in a simple or simplistic faith. The teacher aims to "make knowledge problematic" in this regard, so that as a result, the preacher can "make the case for struggling for a qualitatively better world for all people."[27]

In Christian tradition, what we call "catechesis" or "Christian formation" is quite similar to this idea of critical thinking within community. Indeed, in many ways catechesis fits well within how Thomas Groome thinks about the purposes of Christian education for "shared praxis."[28] Nor are these ideas unlike the posture of preaching-as-teaching from Ron Allen and Tom Long where preaching functions as interpretation for Christian living, which I explored in the introduction. Additionally, we hear resonances with Christian *phronesis*, or wise, faithful Christ living. But whereas Groome limits his work to Christian education and Allen and Long focus on interpretation of the Christian tradition, critical pedagogy turns our eyes toward a different starting place.

Teachers who place themselves within the sphere of critical pedagogy focus on places where suffering and oppression occur, looking to enact emancipatory practice, democratic change, and exercising civic courage. And while I want to underscore that we do not necessarily want to conflate the aims of critical pedagogy and Christian faith, analogues are apparent. The preacher-as-teacher aims to enable the gathered community to approach life with critical thought, then act with emancipatory impulses and courageous love. The womanist theological ethics of Katie Geneva Cannon perfectly captures this approach in her essay, "Womanist Interpretation and Preaching in the Black Church" as she describes how in black preaching

9

"investigation of the integral connection between the preacher who creates the sermon, the sermon's internal design, the world that the sermon reveals, and the religious sensibilities of the congregation that are affected by the sermon *invites us to a higher degree of critical consciousness about the invisible milieu in which we worship.*"[29]

Educator bell hooks's thought is congruent with this notion of approaching education with the goal of critical consciousness. We might almost seamlessly substitute phrasing about preaching:

> Currently, the students I encounter seem far more uncertain about the project of self-actualization than my peers and I were twenty years ago. They feel that there are no clear ethical guidelines shaping actions. Yet, while they despair, they are also adamant that education should be liberatory. They want and demand more from professors than my generation did. There are times when I walk into classrooms overflowing with students who feel terribly wounded in their psyches (many of them see therapists), yet I do not think that they want therapy from me. They do want an education that is healing to the uninformed, unknowing spirit. They do want knowledge that is meaningful. They rightfully expect that my colleagues and I will not offer them information without addressing the connection between what they are learning and their overall life experiences.[30]

With all that is happening in our world that polarizes and wounds, I do not presume that those who fill the pews do not expect a therapeutic aspect to preaching. They do. But in contrast to Fosdick's "project method," which was highly influential in terms of a focus on preaching as counseling, and the kind of prosperity gospel and self-actualization preaching that we see in contemporary preachers like Joel Osteen, the preacher-as-teacher in the mode of critical pedagogy sees the preaching moment as one of liberating transformation that brings healing not just to self, but to fragmented and broken communities and is ambitious enough to work toward the healing of socio-economic and political systems. This is certainly a different sense of preaching-as-teaching: sparking the kind of critical thought that seeks to liberate and bring healing to the world we inhabit together. So the preacher-as-teacher is not simply prophetic preaching under another guise. Personal and social healing, traditionally associated with pastoral preaching, comes under the auspices of the preacher-as-teacher as well.

In a weary, divided world, this kind of critical thought is indispensable. I am reminded of two of my daughter's favorite literary characters: Jack and Annie from The Magic Treehouse series of books. Gender stereotypes aside,

Jack and Annie are quite opposite in how they approach the missions on which they are sent. Jack is wont to painstakingly look through the books he and Annie take on their journeys as a way of prolonging the need to act. Action is not his priority. Annie, on the other hand, acts impulsively, jumping into any situation without a plan and only looks for information later. For the preacher-as-teacher, neither of these is a helpful model, though their types certainly exist in communities of faith of many different social and theological commitments.

Worshipping communities[31] can neither retreat simply to inconclusive spiritual reflection nor engage in knee-jerk actions to issues as they come up. As for the task of addressing taboo topics, contentious and possibly divisive issues, the reimagined preacher-as-teacher empowers pastors to raise before the community those topics and situations that require considerable scrutiny. This is critical thinking at work. Simplicity, silence, or avoidance will not do since the church participates in the wider spheres of public life. Through the lens of critical pedagogy, preachers examine the church's role in taboos and contentious issues, summoning knowledge from a variety of resources, believing that reflection on this knowledge not only can, but must result in emancipatory practices and transformation (which, again, may or may not be directly related to the particular concerns of critical pedagogy).[32]

Transformation

As I noted above, critical pedagogy employs the language of transformation to describe the goals of education. For Giroux, transformation means that teachers "resist the suffocating knowledge and practices that constitute" the social formations of a number of groups.[33] They also seek to "provide the moral, political and pedagogical leadership for those groups which take as their starting point the transformative critique of the conditions of oppression."[34] For critical pedagogy, the teacher works to empower others to bring a more just, more equitable world into being. Educator bell hooks calls this "education as the practice of freedom."[35] Critical thinking in the teaching-learning relationship always has in mind a social end, not merely an inward, individual one.

In North America, critical pedagogy endeavors to help students think critically, then act with courage to work for a more democratic public sphere. As we will see in the chapter on radical imagination, the language of transformation easily merges with (and in many ways emerges from[36]) the Christian vocabulary. So as we reimagine the preacher-as-teacher, a different *telos* will emerge than critical pedagogy's, which points to liberation and emancipation through radical democratic praxis. But all the same, the language of transformation is thoroughly ingrained in the church's language.

Metamorphosis

Perhaps the most familiar cognate for transformation is the term *metamorphosis*. Though not a frequent term in the New Testament, it does occur in key places. Paul's letter to the Romans frames tension between the way things are and the way things should be for the Christian community: "Don't be conformed to the patterns of this world, but be *transformed* by the renewing of your minds so that you can figure out what God's will is—what is good and pleasing and mature" (Romans 12:2). Here Paul describes the character of the Christian life as one of continual transformation toward the godly life. In the mode of critical thinking through critical pedagogy, preachers must ask, "What do we characterize as 'conformation to this world'? What kinds of economic, social, and political powers might lure us to conformation? In a fragmented and weary world, what does God's will look like? And what does it ask of us?"

Two other occurrences of *metamorphosis* in the New Testament need our attention, both from the Pauline literature, both with an eschatological intent. These describe the church's continual transformation into that which we shall ultimately be. Second Corinthians 3:18 says: "All of us are looking with unveiled faces at the glory of the Lord as if we were looking in a mirror. We are being *transformed* into that same image from one degree of glory to the next degree of glory. This comes from the Lord, who is the Spirit." And Philippians 3:21: "[Jesus] will transform our humble bodies so that they are like his glorious body, by the power that also makes him able to subject all things to himself." Clearly, among the many things Paul's letters proclaim, they include the hopeful transformation (1) to which God is calling the church (Romans) and (2) the mysterious work by which God acts to perform salvation of and for the world.

Beyond the specific occurrence of the exact word, we cannot forget the eschatological vision from John of Patmos, who witnesses to the transformation of both the heavens and earth at the consummation of all things (Revelation 21:1). John (or the author) inherits the rhetoric of newness from the Isaiah tradition (65:17; 66:22). This tradition also appears in 2 Peter 3:13, where the Petrine author states "according to [God's] promise we are waiting for a new heaven and a new earth, where righteousness is at home."

Metanoia

Closely related to the familiar word *metamorphosis* is the word *meta-noia*, commonly translated as "repentance," but also carrying the meaning of a change of heart, mind, and thinking, or a turning and change in one's ways. *Metanoia* is at the core of Jesus's own proclamation. The Synoptic Gospels attest to *metanoia* being the opening component of Jesus's ministry. In Matthew, after the arrest of John the Baptist Jesus "began to announce, 'Change your hearts and lives! Here comes the kingdom of heaven!'" (4:17). Of course, John the Baptist first called for *metanoia*, which was rooted in the Old Testament prophetic tradition of calling Israel to repentance. Matthew's language here is that of continuous action. Repentance was not a one-time suggestion by John or Jesus. A call to change endured as a feature of Jesus's ministry. So too in Mark, after Jesus's baptism and desert temptation: "After John was arrested, Jesus came into Galilee announcing God's good news, saying, 'Now is the time! Here comes God's kingdom! Change your hearts and lives, and trust this good news!'" (1:14-15).

In turn, *metanoia* becomes the disciples' ministry of proclamation. In Mark's version of the sending of the Twelve, he tells us "they went out and proclaimed that people should change their hearts and lives" (6:12). Attached to that proclamation was the casting out of demons and the anointing of the sick, resulting in the cure of many (6:13). Repentance forms a key component of Peter's proclamation on the day of Pentecost (Acts 2:38) and a frequent term in the book of Acts as a whole. As many of the Gospel narratives tell us, these preaching-related transformations set people free and launch them into new realities that they could not previously inhabit. Those who were marginalized now find themselves as part of the community. Transformation is not just of the heart, but a liberating new social and theological reality that comes through proclamation of the "good news of God."

In a divided and weary world, preaching that names *metamorphosis* and *metanoia* as central components of both God's salvific work (2 Corinthians and Philippians) and our responsibility as disciples, does the work of teaching—in the sense that critical pedagogy describes teachers as transformative intellectuals. Preaching continually aims for the transformative work that lies at the heart of the good news of God. For as Paul says elsewhere in 2 Corinthians, "So then, if anyone is in Christ, that person is part of the new creation. The old things have gone away, and look, new things have arrived!" (5:17). "New creation" is not merely an inward, pietistic change, though that kind of transformation is certainly not excluded. The Gospel accounts point us to disciples who proclaim a transformed socio-economic and political network. The Revelation to John envisions the ultimate transformation of the cosmos and indeed provides a literary-homiletical intervention in the lives of early Christian communities. This homiletical intervention provides a pattern for the kind of intervention I have been describing, which through the lens of critical pedagogy we are beginning to name as preaching-as-teaching.

Relationship between Theory and Practice

Not unrelated, a self-reflexive dimension is essential in considering the preacher-as-teacher as a transformative intellectual. Critical pedagogy is highly interested in the relationship between theory and practice. Giroux advocates for teachers to be engaged in critical reflection on what political, economic, and social interests emerge through teaching methods and curricula handed down from bureaucratic and institutional sites. Teaching becomes transformative not just because of the kind of content handed over, but because, for the teacher, critical reflection is never divorced from practices in the classroom. As noted above, Giroux sees teachers as "reflective practitioners," not as those who enact "applied science."[37] Here Giroux points to teacher education programs that "call for the separation of conception from execution; the standardization of school knowledge in the interest of managing and controlling it; and the devaluation of critical, intellectual work on the part of teachers and students for the primacy of practical considerations."[38] Here we might think about how many teachers feel compelled simply to teach "to the test" or teach curricula that do not account for student context. Teachers, facing innumerable pressures, simply do as they are told to produce positive statistical results rather than qualitative differences in the lives of their students. As a result, teaching programs and their students become "preoccupied with learning the 'how to,' with 'what works,' or with mastering the best way to teach a *given* body of knowledge."[39] Teaching is thereby reduced to technique, where teachers implement the goals and techniques devised by others (often by those who are not immersed in classrooms on a day-to-day basis). In some very tangible ways, theory stands apart from practice.

The pivot to preaching is easy enough. Think for a moment about what we do as preachers "to be or become more effective." Or consider your own classroom experiences in preaching. What does it mean to preach well, and how is this articulated? How does one learn to do this? If a preacher grows to be more effective, what are the hoped-for outcomes of that effectiveness? When pastors empty their continuing education funds to go to conferences about preaching or to hear great preaching, what are the goals? To learn a new method? To preach without notes or some other aspect of technique? Or simply to be inspired from the draining work of pastoral ministry? Are seminary courses and continuing education about preaching a kind of industrial practice geared toward making preaching "preacher-proof"?[40]

The field of practical theology has had much to say about education for ministry over the past generation. The 1980s brought sharp criticism over the nature of ministerial education that had taken on the so-called clerical paradigm, meaning that education for ministry focused on developing ministerial skills and technical practice at the expense of theory.[41] We might see the parallels to teacher education in this criticism. In response, the theological academy pushed the pendulum (too far in Bonnie Miller-McLemore's estimation) against "clericalism" or ministerial "know-how" toward approaches to ministry grounded in more cognitive, theoretical theological approaches to ministerial education, including preaching. Thus, "reflective practice" has become a byword for all varieties of ministry practice, encouraging ministry practitioners to engage in robust theoretical reflection on practice both prior to and after, creating a kind of practical theological loop.

And yet, despite this robust discussion over the years, ministerial practice in preaching that Giroux might call "technocratic and instrumental rationalities"[42] persists or, as noted above, attempts to make preaching "preacher-proof." Theorizing about preaching gets left out of the equation as the necessity for week-to-week practices that "work" impinge upon time for theoretical reflection on preaching. As many have called it, "the relentless return of Sunday" piles on top of so many other pastoral responsibilities, tempting us to leave out theoretical reflection on the practice of preaching. Who has time to think deeply about the practice of preaching when there are visits to be made, budgets to assess, and, of course, sermons to preach!? So, there are significant discussions about the consistent temptation of plagiarism (who of us has not been tempted or heard of someone in our own ministerial circles who succumbed to plagiarism?). The internet is filled with marketing for sermons for pay, and cookie-cutter templates for preaching method; sermon series are a dime a dozen. I believe that this is not altogether different from the sermon illustration books published over the years for which ministers could simply "plug and play" various material into their own sermons. These kinds of problems are not at all new, but they are indicative of the same kinds of criticisms Giroux makes against teacher education. A note: while we do concern ourselves about method—we can't *not* think about technique in relation to preaching—this can never be the sum total of our own reflection on preaching, lest preaching become purely an instrumental or technical practice.

To bring this full circle, something greater lies beneath this temptation to distance theory from practice. Critical pedagogy might tell us that preaching suffers the same outcome as teaching: a practice rendered mostly innocuous to critical thinking and transformation. So critical thinking is not just the kind of thing that the preacher-as-teacher encourages listeners to do about their lives in connection to the sermon. Informed by critical pedagogy, preacher-as-teachers are encouraged to engage in similar kinds of deep critical thinking about their own preaching practices toward transformed and transformative practice in our complex world.

Conclusion

The preacher-as-teacher is a transformative intellectual: not a dry lecturer satisfied to deliver knowledge to passive or ignorant listeners, but rather one who stands before and with the congregation, authorized to publicly interrogate the contested spheres of church and world, taboos, division, and weariness. Preaching-as-teaching provides an intervention in the lives of those who gather, empowering them for critical thought and work toward various kinds of transformation.

This self-conception prompts several questions to be included in each week's sermon preparation process. The following questions are suggestive, but certainly not exhaustive of the kinds of things the preacher-as-teacher might ask:

a) What does my community know, what do they need to know, and how might that knowledge move them toward critical thought and transformation?

b) Is a kind of hegemonic power at work to keep my community of faith at arm's length from a topic or issue and related biblical text(s), or vice versa?

c) Who or what sets the precedent for silence or conflict, and who benefits by keeping it as such?

d) Why does the reinforcement between public-private apply in this situation but not another?

e) How are we implicated or complicit in the outcome of that silence or conflict?

f) How do I reflect on my own preaching practices, and toward what end(s)?

Returning to the sermon on gun violence I discussed in the introduction, these kinds of questions might have helped the congregation explore why some preferred silence and what political, economic, and cultural forces benefit by the church's silence. They might have helped me more clearly and more quickly assess the political, social, and economic resistances that might have stood in the way of transformation. The preacher-as-teacher seeks to bring to light the power structures that are maintained by silence or conflict. Based on the authority granted from various sources, but most notably the gathered congregation, preaching in the mode of the preacher-as-teacher becomes an authorized intervention in a congregation's common life for the purposes of ecclesial imagination, sharing the resources for formation and flourishing, and inviting listeners into ways of life that reflect the realm of God.

Critical pedagogy imagines the role of teaching as those who contribute to the formation of public life. Teaching is a transformative and intellectual activity that acts as a form of cultural politics. Teachers regularly intervene in the lives of students by teaching emancipatory practices rather than formation of skills or preparation for the workforce. Preaching-as-teaching uses the sermon as an exercise in critical thinking to help the faithful exercise agency in and beyond the ecclesial sphere. The preacher-as-teacher preaches with an aim to enable the gathered community to approach the issues at hand with critical thought, then act with emancipatory impulses and courageous love. And all of this with the public sphere in mind. We now turn to consider the kind of public the preacher-as-teacher envisions.

Chapter Two

The End of Education

Preaching Toward a Public Sphere

> *Pedagogy is always political*
> *because it always presupposes a vision of the future,*
> *legitimizes certain forms of knowledge, values,*
> *and social relations, and in doing so*
> *produces particular forms of agency.*[1]
> —Henry Giroux

In the United States, we have a long-standing, interesting, and complicated relationship between religion and politics. What preacher has not considered the warning about the pulpit becoming "too political"? Those preachers who engage public and perhaps contentious issues in congregations with mixed political party commitments (or what Leah Schade calls "purple congregations") risk alienating their congregants, no matter how lightly they might tread. But in the age of social media, high-volume media coverage, and polarization, the political looms ever larger.[2] In such a world, what relationship does preaching have to the public sphere? I am increasingly worried that preachers in the US context are being driven away from a vision of and for the public good toward a smaller version, limited to addressing the individual and her or his piety or to provide self-help for dynamics of small kinship and community networks or, at most, to speak to the nature of local congregational or denominational systems. The temptation is great to only address the spiritual needs of the individual and, as a by-product, to play into what researcher Christian Smith has dubbed "moral therapeutic deism."[3] David Lose has outlined these dynamics as the effects of secularism: the transcendent, he says, "has been banished to the personal and private dimensions of our lives."[4] At the heart of any congregational resistances to preaching deemed "too political" lies a cultural move to limit the church's role in "the political" as a key player in the collective, public good.

But is the church really the church—the ones "called out" (*ekklesia*)—without a public dimension or without witness to the shape of the public sphere? Is preaching's impact limited to only the personal and individual (which in itself is a problematic dualistic assumption about the separation of individual and public versions of the self)? Is the church really the church if it does not offer a compelling vision for the shape of our common life together? This chapter focuses on how we might envision preaching's authority (and responsibility!) to articulate visions for the public sphere in conversation with the role of the preacher-as-teacher. Informed by critical pedagogy's emphasis on the purposes of education, I will make the case that under the teaching role, preachers have, can, and should preach toward powerful visions of the public sphere, especially fitting for the weary, polarized times in which we find ourselves.

Education with a Public Purpose

There is no such thing as an ideological-neutral or ideology-free education. As the quotation at the beginning of the chapter suggests, the evaluation about the place of ideology and values within education comes as no surprise for those of us who have been swimming in postmodern thought. We know, in fact, that everything is political! Whether we think about it at the elementary, secondary, or undergraduate and graduate levels, education works to produce participants in society-at-large. The question, then, becomes what frameworks inform teachers both in theory and in practice? What versions of public life lie within educational systems, implicitly or explicitly? Whose interests do they serve? What forms of cultural production and life are supported? Who and what is devalued? What purposes does knowledge serve? To some extent, these are questions already raised in the previous chapter with regard to the role of the teacher. But the question about the relationship of Christian preaching to the public sphere is tightly interrelated.

Adherents of critical pedagogy envision teaching as a practice that leads to a certain kind of society. They submit that, at its best, education participates in a "democratic public sphere" where engaged citizens live out deep concern for the welfare of others. Peter McLaren posits that democratic public spheres "encompass networks such as schools, political organizations, *churches*, and social movements that help construct democratic principles and social practices through debate, dialogue, and exchange of opinion."[5] By this, McLaren means that education composes one formative, indispensable component of public life that *includes* religious life. For now, however, we will focus on the role McLaren and other critical pedagogues believe schools play. This network, of which schools are a part, helps form a robust vision of public life that supports democratic principles: a social world in which debate, dialogue, and exchange of opinion shape the backbone of public life rather than the influence of corporate interests (including both the military- and prison-industrial complexes), fear, and retreating tribalisms. As noted previously, education is not only for the purposes of creating a more prepared workforce with certain skills, even as that is a necessary by-product of education, or individual consumers with more purchasing power. Rather, as critical thinkers, the ends of education are an informed, critical, and engaged citizenry.

Giroux goes further, considering how education should promote a kind of "concrete utopianism."[6] By this, Giroux establishes in no uncertain terms that education cannot be divorced from ideology. Education "needs to be informed by a passionate faith in the necessity of struggling to create a better world. In other words, radical pedagogy needs a vision—one that celebrates not what is but what could be, that looks beyond the immediate to the future and links struggle to a new set of human possibilities."[7] And continuing, Giroux presumes that this demand on education is "a call for alternative modes of experience, public spheres that affirm one's faith in the possibility of creative risk-taking, of engaging life so as to enrich it; it means appropriating the critical impulse so as to lay bare the distinction between reality and the conditions that conceal its possibilities."[8]

Now what might this mean in education? Richmond, Virginia, where I teach and live, remains in many ways lodged in its cultural and historical inheritance as the former capital of the Confederacy. Racial and class inequities are deeply ingrained components of daily life in this city. But I was moved by educational experiences my daughter had in her kindergarten class. One day she came home talking about a little girl with "dark skin" who went to school with children with "light skin" whose parents were not happy about this, and who yelled and called her names. She knew the little girl's name: Ruby Bridges. It struck me: I could not recall exactly when I learned Ruby Bridges's name, but I knew it was not until I was much, much older. On another occasion, she had watched at least part of Martin

Luther King Jr.'s "I Have a Dream" speech and came home rehearsing King's hope that one day children of all skin tones could play together. Now it is one thing for a kindergartner to hear King's speech in isolation. But to hear it in concert with the story of Ruby Bridges helped provide context and analysis for why the dream was so pivotal. For a racially mixed school in Richmond, Virginia, this was not just a move to cover the curriculum. Rather, I view this as a pedagogical practice that "links struggle to a new set of human possibilities," re-envisioning the public sphere: that is our social relations in everyday life, which includes economic, cultural, relational, and political spheres of our common existence. And as a corollary, her teacher was working toward a new public sphere as a by-product of envisioning her role as someone who is "struggling to establish a social and economic democracy."[9] In age-appropriate ways, my daughter was learning both social critique and the capacity to act as an active citizen to change the public sphere (both inside her classroom and beyond it), even if she did not have the language for these concepts at the time. This, *in nuce*, is what critical pedagogy might envision as the kind of educational practice that transforms the public sphere.

Preaching Toward a Public Sphere

Similarly, the preacher-as-teacher takes a primary interest in how preaching casts a vision of and for the public sphere. While critical pedagogy makes a case for a certain kind of democratic public sphere, preachers will more often frame the public sphere through the lens of ecclesiology. Each preacher implicitly or explicitly verbalizes the nature of the church and its role in the world. This includes but is not limited to how we define who is part of the church, how the church relates to individual members, how it relates to God, and what role(s) the church plays in the world. To put it simply, how preachers view and express the nature of the church leads to how listeners will frame moral and social issues and how they frame their ideal impact upon, and interaction with, the wider public sphere. If discipleship is not merely belief, but rather "reducing distance" between ourselves and the first disciples whose call to follow Jesus inescapably affected the way they lived their lives, then we cannot help but frame discipleship as interaction with a wider public sphere.[10]

Before going further, I want to make an important distinction. Recognizing that preaching is as much a rhetorical act as it is a theological one, pausing to frame how we think about preaching and the public sphere will be helpful. When I talk about preaching toward a public sphere, I propose that preaching is a communicative event that seeks to construct a vision for the public sphere *beyond* ecclesial gatherings. Of course, preachers will form more internal publics in sermons, which is the congregation itself. This is unavoidable, and we should not desire to avoid it. As Randall Nichols observes, "messages create communities, or, as it is sometimes said in communication jargon, publics."[11] Elsewhere I distinguish these kind of publics as "homiletic communities."[12] The symbols, images, experiences, and stories we employ in sermons have a way of drawing the boundaries of the gathered community: who is in and who is out. We do well to be sensitive to how we construct an internal public sphere in our preaching.[13] In contemporary preaching theory, Wes Allen provides an analysis of the church's preaching conversations. As both description and prescription, Allen believes that preaching should account for a church's overlapping conversations.[14] The internal public of congregations intersects with what Allen calls the "sociohistorical" conversation of the wider world.[15] I do not deny the rhetorical and theological overlap. But what I aim to describe here is not how preaching constitutes the gathered community theologically and rhetorically (how preaching forms the "congregational conversation") but more of a specific theological vision for how the gathered community sees itself *via preaching* in relation to the wider public sphere as arranged in neighborhoods, communities, countries, the world, as well as the institutional and cultural formations constitutive of life within them.

The church's roles in relation to the public sphere have been imagined in different ways. John McClure and Burton Cooper outline the ways each preacher accounts for how she or he believes this relationship takes place, and appropriate H. Richard Niebuhr's categories from his seminal 1951 book *Christ and Culture*.[16] For Cooper and McClure, these categories are as such: (1) The Church against the World, in which the church is called out of the world and its sinful ways, standing in opposition to the ways that the world stands in the contrast to the ways of God by withdrawing from the world. (2) The Church with the World, in which the church gradually realizes God's purposes for the world, working patiently within culture to eliminate sin's consequences with a realistic approach that this will not come quickly or easily. (3) The Church above the World, in which the church recognizes other powers as legitimate, but "works to infuse religious-moral values into all social institutions and actions" in its role as divinely inspired chief among all human institutions. (4) The Church and World in Paradox, which draws from Martin Luther's "two kingdoms," where the church simultaneously recognizes its position as citizens of both the kingdoms of this world and the kingdom of God and must respond with action according with the corresponding kingdom ethic in which one finds themselves at any given moment. (5) The Church as Transformer of the World, in which the church finds a call to deep engagement with, and transformation of, the sinful wider culture.[17]

Nora Tubbs Tisdale invites preachers to be attentive to these dynamics as well, not just in how they are articulated within the sermon, but in how they are expressed by the church in congregational life. As part of the work of "exegeting the congregation," Tisdale advises preachers to pay close attention to the "view of the church," seeking to identify "what metaphors for the church predominate in congregational life," whether the church understands itself to be "a 'hospital for sinners'... or a 'holy community of saints,'" and how inclusive the church is "in its leadership, worship, and programming—of those who are frequently marginalized in the larger society."[18] She continues these questions under a different category, that of "view of Christian mission (evangelism, missiology, social ethics)."[19] Under this heading, Tisdale invites preachers to understand how congregations express their "relation to the larger culture," drawing on Niebuhr's categories. She offers the following possibilities: whether the congregation would be characterized as "activist, civic, evangelistic, or sanctuary," and if the congregation holds the self-image of a "survivor church (reactive to the crises of an overwhelming world), crusader church (proactive in seeking out issues and championing causes), pillar church (anchored in its community and taking responsibility for the community's well-being), pilgrim church (caring for immigrants with ethnic, national, or racial roots), or servant church (caring for and supporting individuals in need)."[20]

In tracing McClure and Cooper's work, as well as Tisdale's, I simply want to note the rich tools available for diagnostic work in identifying the church's relationship with the public sphere. These help preachers recognize that there are a range of theologically grounded options for discerning a homiletic ecclesiology. Perhaps you recognize your own preaching and/or your congregations somewhere within them. Or you might take some time to analyze your past preaching with deeper attention to how the relationship between church and public sphere have emerged in your preaching and congregation. But diagnostic tools are just that. While they raise to the surface a crucial awareness of what one might be doing, they do not necessarily advocate for a position vis-à-vis the church and the public sphere.

Homiletical Options for Imagining the Public Sphere

So how might the preacher-as-teacher imagine the public sphere, and the church's relationship to it, through the lens of critical pedagogy? Through this frame, preachers will seek to voice a kind of ecclesiology that imagines the public sphere as one in which the church has vigorous inter-action, seeking a highly participatory role where social action and change stand at the forefront. No doubt, we can see here various liberation theologies already advocating this kind of preaching: transformation of theologically and socially oppressive structures toward liberation for both oppressed and oppressor. I have previously noted the connection between Paulo Freire and Latin American liberation theology. Contemporary voices like Peter McLaren continue that connection, even as the work has necessarily changed for this context. Just as critical pedagogy has had to appropriate critical pedagogy differently in the North American context, neither does there exist a straight-line model of application appropriate for much of the mainstream, privileged church in North America. We will need to imagine some new, more appropriate possibilities, particularly within the current highly polarized context. Many preachers are often asked about (or they themselves question) the relationship between the pulpit and the political. Some fear what has come to be known as "prophetic preaching." The wider body of preaching literature presents some helpful options that have resonances with critical pedagogy.

In Charles Campbell's *The Word Before the Powers* the preacher serves as one who unmasks the "Powers" that shape the world as it is while calling forth both their transformation and ours.[21] In this model, Campbell appropriates the work of Walter Wink, offering a spiritually sensitive etiology of the "Powers." Campbell prioritizes three commitments: (1) Preaching takes place within the realm of the biblically titled "principalities and pow-ers" that seek to work death in the world. These powers stand in conflict to the word of God. (2) Preaching functions effectively as a major practice of resistance, certainly through the content of its message, but also as the very act of speaking becomes an act of nonviolent resistance. (3) The church engages the powers as a community of resistance, formed by its own "pe-culiar practices and virtues."[22] We can effectively qualify this within the realm of what McClure and Cooper call "the Church as Transformer of the World." With the third component particularly in mind, preaching's focus is resistance and forming a preaching-shaped (in addition to various other church-centered practices) community of resistance.

As Campbell acknowledges, his focus centers on developing "an ethic of preaching," built upon "exposing" and "unmasking" the Powers. Campbell gives disproportionately meager attention to what I have been calling a vision for the public sphere.[23] He calls preachers to attend to "tokens of the resurrection," instances of "God's Shalom that [are] already breaking into the world."[24] And additionally, he invites preachers to practice "disjunctive vision," which entails "audaciously holding before the congregation a vision of the new creation that is coming, even when there is no evidence for it in the present."[25] But he gives these scant treatment. And why should they receive more? When one is so heavily invested in the church's identity as a contrast community characterized chiefly by nonviolent resistance, hope in "God's purposes for the world enables us to wait patiently to resist the powers of death without . . . having to control the future through acts of violence."[26] Eschatological hope and worship practices become both sustaining practice and primary acts (though, to be fair, not the only ones) by which Christian communities negotiate the grip the Powers exert on the world. And though it may not be true for Campbell, this line of thought risks becoming a sectarian vision where the church withdraws from the public sphere in some significant ways.[27]

Operating in a different mode, Kenyatta Gilbert examines African American preaching from the period of the Great Migration. Guided by "the resolute conviction that listeners in their northern Black congregations needed a way to articulate their misery and be free from America's created 'cultures of silence,'" Gilbert shows how preachers like Adam Clayton Powell Sr. and others preached in such a way as to help their communities develop a vision of a public sphere characterized by political, economic, and social equality.[28] Gilbert's study infuses the discussion of preaching toward a vision of the public sphere with a much-needed historical consciousness. For "the Exodus preaching paradigm," African American prophetic preaching began with the highly contextualized socio-cultural realities of oppressed Black American citizens and, "by not retreating from daunting issues of the public sphere, prophetic Black preaching sought to expose America's failed promises to its Black citizens. . . . Because a few Black clerics dared to preach prophetically, many heard the promise of a new and hopeful future in their urban Promised Land."[29] Gilbert goes on to characterize the preaching of this era as equally willing to name places in the public sphere with "either holy graciousness or holy judgment."[30] As such, African American preaching in this era named a vision of the public sphere in which

African Americans were included as full and free citizens on American life, calling into judgment the places where that vision was being denied and how new social realities might begin to emerge. I am highly appreciative of Gilbert's work in this regard, and indeed in the next chapter I will highlight some further similarities in his use of the work of Paulo Freire. But in my appreciation, I also want to be careful not to unjustly appropriate that highly contextual model for communities who may have different historical, cultural, and social realities. It is sufficient at this point to name the resonances that Gilbert's homiletical model has with what I describe below and the historical significance of its emergence in a specific time and place and for a specific people.

We might also consider the recent public preaching of William J. Barber II, who has served in many ways as the public voice of the Moral Monday Movement in North Carolina for the past several years. More recently, he has expanded his work to the new Poor People's Campaign, a grassroots effort to continue the legacy of Martin Luther King Jr.'s later years. While some might consider Barber's preaching to be "political," Barber's preaching operates without partisan agenda.[31] In fact, Barber espouses a multifaith moral movement that seeks specific goals for a public sphere that acknowledges human interconnectedness toward five human values: equitable economic structures, educational equality, health care for all, criminal justice reform and equality, and equal protections for voting.[32] These values have more recently been named in the Poor People's Campaign as systemic racism, poverty, the war economy, ecological devastation, and the nation's distorted morality.[33] Barber's preaching advocates for a broader movement with a specific vision of the public sphere and indeed of the nation, with the hope that the nation will "live out its highest principles."[34] As opposed to Campbell's virtuous, contrast worshipping community, Barber's preaching advocates for a highly integrated, highly visible faith movement in the public square that reaches beyond traditional confines of church, synagogue, mosque, and other congregational formations. This preaching begins with a slate of public values that forms the core vision of a just, equitable public sphere. But the kind of preaching in which Barber engages on the public stage may not be sustainable or appropriate in the long-term for week-to-week congregational preaching in Christian congregations (even if Barber still preaches regularly in the congregation where he serves as pastor). Barber's preaching is compelling, but it does not address the full realm of experiences with which a congregation deals in its week-to-week life. Barber's preaching in that mode is meant to be on the public stage, rather than behind the pulpit in the same church every Sunday. It leans on consistent social action in which civil disobedience and arrest come to the fore more often than not.

So while there are things to admire in each of these models, Campbell's vision of the public sphere is fueled by a kind of internal focus, Gilbert's description of preaching in the Great Migration era might not have broader applicability, and Barber's homiletic interaction with the public sphere is not sustainable for individual congregations over the long term, even as it is undergirded by the prophetic tradition of the Hebrew Bible. We have not yet found a way to imagine the public sphere in our preaching that fits many of our congregational settings.

Imagining the Public Sphere through the *Basileia tou Theou*

Critical pedagogy might recommend that the preacher-as-teacher consider a kind of ecclesiology in which the transformation of culture, bold social action, and commitment to social change stand at the forefront. This kind of preaching is best framed by imagining the public sphere through the language of *basileia tou Theou* (a Greek phrase in the New Testament variously interpreted as: kingdom, dominion, reign, realm, and rule of God) lived and proclaimed through Jesus Christ.

In articulating a vision of the public square in preaching, our preaching can again be fueled by the notion of the *basileia tou Theou*. David Buttrick has drawn out an operating theological foundation rooted in the preaching of Jesus. As Buttrick notes, "in triumphalist eras, we seem to get high Christologies, whereas in transitional moments when societies must change, the gospel of the kingdom is once more spoken. In the twentieth century, with the rise of neo-orthodoxy, we embraced a high Christology. Preachers preached Christ as the only savior, although often without any social content. Now in a time of revolutionary change, once more the church may need recover the good news of God's promised social order."[35]

While Buttrick published those words in 1998, they are strikingly fresh for our time when totalitarianism and authoritarian voices rise, when violence lurks, and when people are so intensely divided as much in social media as they seem to be in the polls and in other areas of cultural life. We do find ourselves amid revolutionary change. And what Buttrick wants us to hear again with fresh ears is the social and theological vision inherent to the *basileia tou Theou*. Jesus did not preach himself, which is what Buttrick points to when he talks about the insufficiency of preaching a high Christology. He continually pointed to the *basileia tou Theou* as the measure by which life should be lived and in which eternal things are bound.

Admittedly, we must be careful with this language, which is why at some points I will use only the Greek transliteration. The term has been variously translated through the years and in recent years with particular sensitivity to issues of colonialism and patriarchy. So, in an effort to be more just in our preaching and liturgical language, we employ alternative terms like *kin-dom*, which I often use in certain settings. But we are still at a loss with this term in a time such as this, when nationalistic language and power are employed so strategically, when militarism runs rampant, when would-be leaders demand fealty, and each of those creep into church discourse and practice. While we can be sensitive to the overtones that a term like *kingdom* might entail, we also need to be responsive to the language and impulses inherent to Jesus's use of the term in the context of the Roman empire.[36]

So what do Buttrick and others see in the *basileia tou Theou*? How might it help our preaching to cast a compelling vision for the public sphere?

Buttrick and Brian Blount unpack historical understandings of the phrase *kingdom of God* (interestingly enough, both were published in the same year).[37] Buttrick and Blount carefully narrate the pitfalls of different turns in the history of this term. These are helpful taxonomies for our attention. The liberal theology movement in the late nineteenth and early twentieth centuries placed its confidence in the progressive dream that "the kingdom of God was regarded as a human project soon to be fulfilled. Either the kingdom would be won by moral endeavor or the world was a mission field where the kingdom would be realized evangelically as pagan peoples were converted—'the kingdom of God in our generation' was a popular slogan."[38] This movement captures the confidence of German theologian Albrecht Ritschl and the American Social Gospel movement led in the twentieth century by Walter Rauschenbusch. And in retrospect, we recognize that the confidence and optimism of this position was forced to retreat with the onset of both world wars.

Blount and Buttrick pivot next to what Buttrick calls the "unpreachable" Jesus of early-twentieth-century biblical scholarship, particularly that of Albert Schweitzer and Johannes Weiss. Unlike their predecessors, they saw Jesus as an apocalyptic prophet, where though Jesus "expected [the kingdom's] imminent arrival, it was wholly future and beyond all human control, even his own as Son of man. Only God could and would broker it."[39] We might think here of Jesus as the street-corner, sandwich-board donning preacher, wild-eyed and shouting about God's future, which was then, as it is today, unpalatable for would-be sermon listeners and Jesus followers.

In response to these came the rise of neo-orthodoxy, with its broad emphases on human sinfulness and God's historical self-revelation in the person of Jesus Christ. The kingdom was no longer a human possibility, as it was with liberal theology, but rather a historical event-in-time located in the work of Jesus Christ. For neo-orthodoxy, "there is no future newness [which characterized Jesus's own preaching], for everything is merely the outworking of the Christ event. Neo-orthodoxy, in which most of us have been formed, redefined revelation and in so doing undercut the social image of the kingdom of God."[40] In characterizing neo-orthodoxy and the biblical theology's effect on preaching, Buttrick asks if historical revelation located in the biblical world took the place of the future-oriented kingdom of Jesus's own preaching. And so Buttrick laments, "somehow the future of God disappeared."[41]

Blount focuses more discretely on biblical interpretation and how others approach the now-possibilities and future-hopes of the kingdom. And for Blount, Norman Perrin's naming of the kingdom of God as a "tensive symbol" is helpful. By using this term, Perrin argues that rather than limiting what the kingdom of God meant to Jesus and to contemporaries, the range of possibilities for the meaning of the kingdom of God expand. And as a result, "the kingdom could represent both present and future realities, ethical and existential conceptualities, be wholly other and yet presently realized at the same time."[42] So rather than limiting the kingdom of God exclusively to either a social sphere of human endeavor (as he cautions later with liberation theology) or an existential one built on God's future (we might also add Buttrick's criticism of the historical Christ-event here), Blount believes that the two can hold together in the fuller understanding of the kingdom of God.

So, what are we to make of the kingdom of God then? What role does it play in shaping a vision of the public sphere in preaching? Remember that the teacher informed by critical pedagogy begins with a reasoned *telos* of a thoroughly democratic public sphere free of oppression, where reordered relationships shape education. So too with those that begin with the *telos* of the kingdom of God: a vision of God's future. In doing so, according to Buttrick, "we will preach social vision. We will picture a redeemed social world, and invite our people to come join God's new humanity."[43] This is radically different from the liberal theological vision of progress. And it is different from the inward-looking salvation of the individual. So too for

Blount, who examines the kingdom of God through the lens of the Gospel of Mark. He contends:

> Preaching, particularly the preaching of Jesus about the kingdom, acts as the literary mechanism through which God's future kingdom power intervenes in the present moment. Jesus' proclamation is an event which in its very speaking inaugurates, at least in the form of a present pocket, the thing it declares, the imminently coming kingdom. It is not, however, an act/event unique to Jesus. His preaching is presented by Mark as both the successor to John's proclamation of God's intervention through him, and the prototype for the preaching of those who follow him as disciples. Their contemporary preaching in the Markan community is to do what Jesus' preaching did a generation before, establish the kingdom of God as a "pocket" that resists the oppressive social, religious and political boundaries that litter the landscape of human living.[44]

This is a thoroughly public and social vision for preaching, worthy of the moment in which we find ourselves. To preach personal salvation as a future-only option can be a form of escapism. To preach liberal confidence in human efforts to build the present kingdom of God ignores a (future) reality beyond human control. Both of these options miss the mark of Jesus's own preaching. And yet they populate pulpits far and wide. I noted above the dates of Blount and Buttrick's work earlier (1998) because I believe that this emphasis and understanding of the kingdom of God has somehow eluded much of our preaching. And indeed, the kingdom of God seems not to have been a focus for the past twenty years in preaching literature.

At the risk of vastly oversimplifying things, each semester in my introductory preaching class, without fail I am approached by students who experience a crippling fear in preaching their first sermon from the Hebrew Bible and Old Testament. They will ask timidly and almost in hushed tones or by e-mail, as if they are about to engage in heretical scandal, asking, "Can I preach this text without preaching Jesus?" To which I usually reply, "What did Jesus preach? Himself? The biblical text? Or the kingdom of God?" The obvious answer, of course, is the kingdom of God. Somehow we have grown allergic to proclaiming the vision of the kingdom of God, and as a result, our congregational capacities to envision the public sphere have suffered. Instead we settle for the weak vision for the public sphere of both sides of the history of interpretation of the term. I contend that what can save our preaching (again) in these wearisome times is the kingdom of God, the kingdom that Jesus came preaching. As Blount indicates, our very discipleship depends on that mandate to preach the kingdom.

When we proclaim a vision of the kingdom of God, we inherently proclaim a version of the public sphere that becomes entirely reordered from its present state and that offers a compelling invitation to live now into the shape of God's future. When we "seek first the kingdom of God" in our preaching, we will honestly confront our present situation with the truth that God-with-us calls us to reorient our lives to one another: in our networks of personal relationship, our social relationships, our economic lives, our political sensibilities, and our values as community and nation. And yet we recognize the call to (and possibility of) repentance as well as the times and places where we do glimpse God's yet-to-be in the here-and-now, even as we rely on a future hope. And we call on those who gather week to week to live more and more as participants of the kingdom, in many ways just as critical pedagogy calls individuals to work together toward a vision of democracy.

This is part of what makes Martin Luther King Jr.'s "I Have a Dream" speech, as well as his other speeches and sermons, so compelling. King's preaching reminds us that "it is in the transformative, boundary-breaking preaching that the future kingdom of God becomes a present pocket for both Jesus and those who follow him."[45] This means recognizing that the intervention of the kingdom of God is bound up with all the ways that our relationships are ordered in the public sphere. And I want to make plain that the language in the title of this chapter is not incidental: we preach *toward* a public sphere. Inasmuch as the reality of the kingdom of God has "drawn near" in and through Jesus, we preach our communities and congregations in that direction: growing ever closer to the vision of the public sphere inherent to the kingdom of God. The kingdom of God is about moving ourselves, our churches, our institutions, and all the relationships that govern our lives in the direction of the renewed public sphere, even as God acted and continues to act independently of our most faithful intentions.

Preaching toward this public sphere calls forth some specific preaching practices from us. In approaching the week-to-week work of preaching, I think a few key questions are particularly important to add to our usual list of preaching tasks.

First, it is important to ask, "What vision for the public sphere is impressed upon my listeners through their present relationships, institutions, and systems of influence?" Understanding this vision or more likely, multiple visions, and the impact they have upon our listeners grants us a contextual understanding of how our preaching-as-teaching provides an intervention and exercises critical thinking, as described in the previous chapter.

Second, we might ask of the particular biblical passage(s) in front of us, "What kind of vision for the public sphere is envisioned in this biblical text?" Or asked a bit more specifically, "What kind of relationships between people and institutions are called forth as I understand the intentions of this biblical text? Are they consistent with the kingdom of God?"[46] And as many critical interpreters will remind us, we do well to harbor the possibility that the intentions of biblical texts may not always be benevolent toward subjugated persons or groups.

Additionally, from time to time preachers should ask an evaluative sort of question like, "What kind of vision of/for the public sphere have I been working toward through my preaching?" Proponents of critical pedagogy prompt us to ask this question. What is the *telos* of our preaching? Does it fall to the existential and spiritual individual side? Or to the side of human possibility? Are there ways that my preaching has been complicit in upholding a vision for the public sphere that does not adhere to my understanding of God's *telos*? What gaps are present? What adjustments need to be made to be more faithful in the future?

To summarize these three, in preparing to preach we should ask:

1. What's the vision for the public sphere in my congregation?
2. What's the vision for the public sphere in the biblical text?
3. What's the vision for the public sphere in my preaching and this sermon?

I do not assume that these questions complete the loop for us. As a matter of fact, the character of the public sphere and our interaction with it as I've described it thus far has been somewhat vague. In the next chapter, I want to describe some characteristics of our preaching and interaction with the public sphere that add texture to the work of reimagining the preacher-as-teacher through the lens of critical pedagogy.

Chapter Three
Strategies of the Preacher-as-Teacher

Critique, Possibility/Hope, and Radical Imagination

Unveil opportunities for hope no matter what the obstacles might be.
After all, without hope, there is little we can do.[1]
—Paulo Freire, *Pedagogy of Hope*

C losely intertwined with the fact that we are working toward some version of the public sphere in our preaching, the preacher-as-teacher knows that such public spheres entail calling forth the practices of critique, possibility/hope, and imagination. For critical pedagogy, these are practices, or perhaps better put, "modes" of teaching practice, which are deeply ingrained in the practices of teaching. And not only are they teaching practices, but they are part and parcel of the desired outcome for students. In this mode, education bypasses the ostensibly value-neutral goals of information transmission. Instead, this triune understanding of teaching looks at the present public sphere, seeks to name its faults, but not to be content with the way things are, articulates possibility/hope, and cultivates "radical imagination." This chapter seeks to unpack how these pedagogical practices or modes align with a vision of the preacher-as-teacher.

The Radical Imagination
in Critical Pedagogy

For Giroux, bell hooks, and others, education articulates both critique and the possibility of hope. In the mode of critique, Giroux "examine[s] the various ways in which classrooms too often function as modes of social, political, and cultural reproduction.... In the context of reproductions, pedagogy is largely reduced to a transmission model of teaching and limited to the propagation of a culture of conformity and the passive absorption of knowledge."[2] With even a passing familiarity with the work of Paulo Freire, we see his influence in Giroux's words. Critique seeks to uncover the ways that classrooms (by which Giroux uses a shorthand for whole educational systems) simply seek to pass on the virtues of dominant cultures and disempower or allow to remain disempowered those who would bring forth transformational change. Especially important in this mode of critique is identification of how "traditional pedagogy operate[s] under the sway of technical mastery, instrumental logic, and various other fundamentalisms that acquire their authority by erasing any trace of subaltern histories, class struggles, and racial and gender inequalities and injustices."[3] That is admittedly a bigger bite to chew. What Giroux means here is that traditional teaching methods and educational systems are designed in such a way to produce students who, in common parlance, "are prepared for the workforce" or who can "get a good job." The important thing in the reigning practices of schooling is to reproduce the social, political, and cultural norms that exist now, not to produce students capable of calling into question how they came to be and how they propagate their existence by inequalities. In such an education, students are left critically unaware (or numb to) how our globalizing industrial cultures mask histories and current realities of injustices imposed upon various groups.

In exploring the traditional role of the university in the United States, bell hooks observes that "in pursuit of truth and the sharing of knowledge and information, it is painfully clear that biases that uphold and maintain white supremacy, imperialism, sexism, and racism have distorted education so that it is no longer about the practice of freedom."[4] Instead, educational systems and pedagogical practices seek to reinscribe patterns of patriarchy and other forms of domination by selling the vision of a job as the *telos* of education. Thus, hooks recognizes that "the education most of us had received and were giving was not and is never politically neutral."[5]

Critical pedagogy does not stop with critique. Rather, it also moves in the mode of what Giroux interchangeably calls "possibility" and "hope." As such, critical pedagogy becomes a way of "address[ing] the democratic potential of engaging how experience, knowledge, and power are shaped in the classroom in different and often unequal contexts, and how teacher authority might be mobilized against dominant pedagogical practices as part of the practice of freedom."[6] Teachers then see past the limitations of pedagogical practices that reinscribe domination and seek ways that support democratic freedom. Again, a certain kind of public sphere is envisioned through teaching practices: a more just, equitable, and free society that works toward the end of oppression and suffering, reaching toward freedom shared by all. This means that teachers interrogate curriculum, teaching practices, and bureaucratic models of education and come out on the other side with a different vision. For bell hooks, this consists of the hopes that teaching, or rather education as a whole, can be "the practice of freedom"[7] such that students have "the capacity to live fully and deeply."[8] As Giroux says in multiple places through his work, the goal for education becomes to "make despair unconvincing and hope practical."[9]

To do this, critical educators nurture what Giroux and others have called the "radical imagination." Imagination is no simple category, having been used in popular renderings as the capacity to call images and memories to mind. Imagination constitutes a vital component of creativity. But for critical pedagogy, imagination has significant complexity, moral underpinnings, and political purpose. Imagination can be formed and used for benevolent purposes as well as sinister ones. Political theorist Hannah Arendt, whose work around totalitarianism is picked up by critical pedagogy, grants substantial meaning to imagination. For Arendt, political action in the world "consists of the capacity to imagine this future world in which new beginnings will find expression without losing grasp of the world as it still is."[10] This dimension of the imagination holds potential for critical pedagogy.

When teachers and learners together cultivate radical imagination, they begin to envision ways toward the renewed public sphere. Giroux believes "spaces that promote a radical imaginary are crucial in a democracy because they are foundational for developing those formative cultures necessary for youth and old alike to develop the knowledge, skills, and values central to democratic forms of education, engagement, and agency."[11] Again, whereas dominant forms of education place the emphasis of education on workforce development and technical skills to (eventually) maximize productivity and profits for corporate structures, critical and radical educators seek spaces of teaching and learning where students acquire an education that enables

37

their critical thinking, valuation of individuals within society, and critical citizenship that seeks the good of all rather than the few.

Radical imagination requires the capacity to see beyond current frameworks of teaching and learning as well as the *telos* of education. Eric J. Weiner raises some crucial questions in this regard:

> Have we lost the capacity (or have we ever possessed it) to imagine beyond that which we know? If we can get beyond that which we already know, will this process be helpful to people who are personally suffering the implications of impersonal and often violent social, political, economic, and cultural forces? This is a fundamental question—a radical question—on which the entire project [of critical pedagogy] rests; for if it becomes just another exercise in theory, then it cannot be said to be a rejuvenation or resignification of anything, let alone a critical imaginary. Rewriting categories of the real in an effort to jump-start the imagination has to, in the end, offer real people in real situations real tools by which they (we) can make their (our) lives more free.[12]

Notice how Weiner talks about education. This is not an enterprise of high-stakes testing culture, graduation rates, workforce preparation, and technical rationality. Neither is this imagination just an exercise in theory. For Weiner and critical pedagogy, education has the capacity to imagine beyond current conditions and educate toward practices for freedom where citizens work together to eliminate the forces that impose violence and oppression. Notice further how Weiner's language borders on the numinous and even apocalyptic when he describes the practices of imagining "beyond that which we know" and "rewriting the categories of the real." This is not just ambitious, but instead pushes those of us with theological sensibilities to think about our practices of ministry.

Two further concepts are important with regard to the radical imagination, as described by Giroux. He does not back away from what we might very well call apocalyptic language with regard to these concepts as they relate to radical imagination. The first is what Giroux describes as the "disimagination machine," which he borrows from Georges Didi-Huberman. By this, Giroux

> refers to images . . . institutions, discourses, and other modes of representation, that undermine the capacity of individuals to bear witness to a different and critical sense of remembering, agency, ethics and collective resistance. The "disimagination machine" is both a set of cultural apparatuses extending from schools and mainstream media to the new sites of screen culture, and a public pedagogy that function primarily to

undermine the ability of individuals to think critically, imagine the un-imaginable, and engage in thoughtful and critical dialogue: put simply, to become critically informed citizens of the world.[13]

Giroux sees the "disimagination machine" as an interconnected network of political, economic, social, and cultural forces at work in education "in the service of creating a neoliberal, dumbed-down workforce."[14] In some broad categories, the "disimagination machine" extends its destructive reach through curriculum and textbook decisions, legislative agendas, and media outlets.

Related, and secondly, Giroux often describes schools as "dead zones of the imagination." In doing so, Giroux points to the corporate influence on schools that seek to disempower public schools so that they become "anti-public spaces that wage an assault on critical thinking, civic literacy and historical memory."[15] Rather than fostering critical citizenship and engaged critical thinking, public schools are becoming "testing hubs" that harshly affect both students and teachers by rendering them both as mere measurable gains and losses. And they are being "refigured as punishment centers" that disproportionately affect minority and low-income students. What matters in education is "memorization, conformity, passivity, and high stakes testing. Rather than create autonomous, critical, and civically engaged students… [S]chools teach confusion by ignoring historical and relational contexts. Every topic is taught in isolation and communicated by way of sterile pieces of information that have no shared meanings or contexts."[16] This is understandably problematic, and Giroux speaks in such glaring terms to bring our awareness to the sweeping networks of power and capital that work to make the "dead zones of the imagination" a reality. And yet, Giroux, hooks, and others do not believe we are anchored to these realities. Radical imagination and education as a practice of freedom point toward another way. All is not lost. Giroux advises that teachers and cultural workers can still press back:

> The radical imagination can be nurtured around the merging of critique and hope, the capacity to connect private troubles with broader social considerations, and the production of alternative formative cultures that provide the precondition for political engagement and for energizing democratic movements for social change—movements willing to think beyond isolated struggles and the limits of a savage global capitalism.[17]

For the preacher-as-teacher, critique, possibility/hope, and radical imagi-nation are vital components of the kind of preaching that works to press toward a new public sphere in the mold of the realm of God.

The Radical Imagination
in Christian Preaching

As we consider the preacher-as-teacher through the lens of the radical imagination, it's important to state that I'm aware that these practices are already happening in preaching and in published work that precedes me. In fact, in what follows, I will point to the illuminative work that accomplishes these very tasks. What I think is important, however, is that our current time compels us to *frame these practices differently*, and that the preacher-as-teacher is a suitable frame. As I've proposed throughout the book, while I think terms such as *resistance* and *prophetic* to describe our preaching are important, these phrases may be worn thin in a time of cultural division and religious fatigue. To fold them into an image of the preacher that is widely embraced gives a more holistic sense of preaching, rather than piecemeal, occasional, or even oppositional and combative. Prophets pop up from time to time as needed and may wear out their welcome or their situation (like pastoral whack-a-mole!), depending upon the circumstance. Even further, the temptation endemic to the prophetic image of preaching places the preacher over, against, or in opposition to the people (or to their beliefs or to the ways that they are being held captive, and so on). The problem is one of distance and difference, even when one adopts a "pastoral approach."[18] But the teacher endures, covering a wide variety of concerns. The teacher stands no less concerned about the issues the prophet addresses, no less passionate about the things that matter, no less willing to speak daringly, but frames her preaching ministry as a whole through a unified lens. Again, the goal is to avoid fragmentation of preaching identity, so that preaching that addresses taboos or difficult topics are not irregular occurrences or out of keeping with preaching identity expressed elsewhere. For the remainder of this chapter, I will outline the ways the preacher-as-teacher might work toward expressions of critique, possibility/hope, and radical imagination.

Radical Imagination

For reasons that will become clear below, I want to start with the radical imagination as a practice or mode of the preacher-as-teacher. To begin, when we think about preaching and the imagination, we have to make some differentiation with regard to what we're talking about. One of the most significant uses of the term imagination in preaching might be called the "poetic imagination."[19] Poetics in preaching concerns itself with the kind of language used for preaching. It "comprises the theory of language use, figures of speech, strategies of form, arrangement, and performance. Preachers must decide not only what they will say but also how they will say it, and it is here that poetics both assists and challenges."[20] Alternatively, "creativity" might be an appropriate substitute for imagination in this sense. In a sense, poetic imagination seeks to find evocative language for sermon listeners' theological understanding.[21] For Thomas Troeger, this kind of imagination "uses the powers of observation to become receptive to the Holy Spirit, who works upon our consciousness through patterns of association and juxtaposition."[22] Most of us know how this kind of imagination works as preachers, whether we feel that we excel at it or not. Poetic imagination is cultivated; we give it permission to operate in the background of our constantly running homiletic processors. So when Barbara Brown Taylor walks down the street, she sees

> a wild-looking character sitting on the steps of the library. His gray hair is matted. His dense beard covers the slogan on his grimy T-shirt. His small darting eyes are as volatile as a hawk's. I look once and think "drifter." I look twice and think "John the Baptist," and in that imaginative act my relationship to the man is changed.[23]

Two things operate simultaneously here. First, as Troeger notes, a pattern of association and juxtaposition places the man on the street in a comparative relationship with the biblical character John the Baptist. The imagination acts to make an association between the biblical world and our own. Second, as Taylor notes, through the poetic imagination her own relationship to the man changes. While she does not say how or why (employing our own use of imagination!), we might posit that Taylor means an ethical change. Whereas she might have passed him by before, the juxtaposition of John the Baptist to her current context might now open her up to receiving something significant the man has to say.

If we think about this from the viewpoint of critical pedagogy, we might say that the temptation for poetic imagination to remain at the level of juxtapositions and associations, naïve to the fact that these are in no way value-neutral associations. In a sense, this would comprise the kind of technical rationality akin to the skills students in schools learn to read and write poetry or short stories because it is a genre of literature with specific features mandated by the state or district standards of learning, rather than how poems or short stories function as literature of protest or social commentary. In that sense, learning about poetry or prose are for reproduction of valueless knowledge or vapid entertainment rather than cultivating these arts as a critical component of embodied, enacted life as people of faith.

While this capacity to employ the poetic imagination is an indispensable component of preaching, the imagination functions in an even more significant way. Barbara Brown Taylor's second observation points us toward what Thomas Troeger calls "the visionary imagination," which among other things, helps the preacher in the task of "identifying the holiest dreams at the heart of God."[24] Paul Ricoeur describes this kind of imagination as "seeing as," which empowers human action, rather than remaining a cognitive kind of activity.[25] Here the preaching of the Hebrew Bible's prophets and Jesus's vision of the *basileia tou Theou* come into play. Their poetic imagination stokes what we are calling the radical imagination, as the associations and juxtaposition of their preaching serve to imagine the world otherwise. Through images, stories, and parables the poetic imagination found within the Bible serves God's greater purposes.

Others have described the radical imagination, and their descriptions should certainly impact our own understanding. The most notable of these comes to us through Old Testament scholar Walter Brueggemann in his classic work *The Prophetic Imagination* and follow-up text *The Practice of Prophetic Imagination: Preaching an Emancipating Word.*[26] For those familiar with Brueggemann's work, the similarities in language are likely already apparent. For Brueggemann, "the task of prophetic ministry is to nurture, nourish, and evoke a consciousness and perception alternative to the consciousness and perception of the dominant culture around us."[27] In his later text, he says of preaching in particular that "prophetic preaching is an act of imagination that is propelled and funded by the previous acts of imagination in the normative story of Israel that evokes YHWH as defining character and agent."[28] For Brueggemann, the stories of the Hebrew Bible fund an imagination that operates otherwise to dominant oppressive cultures.

In *The Prophetic Imagination*, Brueggemann locates the origination of the prophetic imagination in the story of God's work through Moses and the exodus of the Hebrew people from slavery. The work of prophetic imagination is created and sustained by the disclosure of "the alternative religion of the freedom of God" in which there is an "emergence of a new social community in history, a community that has historical body, that had to devise laws, patterns of governance and order, norms of right and wrong, and sanctions of accountability. The participants in the Exodus found themselves, undoubtedly surprisingly to them, involved in the intentional formation of a new social community to match the vision of God's freedom."[29] In other words, the vision they find in God's reality funds their imagination of another way of being in relationship with one another as a community as well as with those they will encounter along the way. Here is the significant point of deviation from critical pedagogy. Whereas radical imagination for critical pedagogy is funded by a version of democracy, radical imagination for the preacher-as-teacher is funded by core understandings of the nature, activity, presence, and purpose of God, particularly in remembering God's faithful past. Thus, while there may be some resonances between preaching and advocacy speech in the public sphere (or the work of critical pedagogy within educational institutions), there is a dividing line that settles on the God we find mediating covenant with Israel in sacred scripture and who we find active in the person of Jesus of Nazareth.

To sharpen this concept, Brueggemann describes an analogous relationship: for preachers, as it was for the prophets and for Jesus, imagination means "the capacity to generate and enunciate images of reality that are not rooted in the world in front of us. Thus, imagination moves outside the box of the given and the taken for granted."[30] That is to say, the poetic imagination and the radical or prophetic imagination work in tandem to evoke the new social order at the heart of God. Repeatedly, Brueggemann invites a kind of mimesis of the prophets' poetry, which while "concretely resonant with the real, situated life of Israel in the world" was "at the same time, slightly removed, in their edgy way, from didactic specificity about public issues."[31] He goes on to characterize how this kind of poetics and elusiveness made it so that the powerful could not use it in their service.[32] We might naturally think about the language of Ezekiel, Daniel, and Revelation. At first glance, Brueggemann's commitment to lack of specificity about public issues might seem a bit unnerving. But at the same time, Brueggemann acknowledges that "prophetic speech . . . is concrete talk in particular circumstances where the larger purposes of God for the human enterprise come down to the particulars of hurt and healing, of despair and hope. . . . What we have to say is rooted in textual memory and is driven by present pain."[33] The poetic imagination and the radical imagination indeed come together for Brueggemann.

Likewise, womanist theologian Kelly Brown Douglas proposes "moral imagination" in connection to the kingdom of God and "black bodies." For Brown Douglas, "a moral imagination disrupts the notion that the world as it is reflects God's intentions. With a moral imagination one is able to live proleptically, that is, as if the new heaven and new earth were already here. This means one's life is not constrained by what is. It is oriented toward what will be."[34] As she draws from Martin Luther King Jr.'s ministry and public speech, she ties in the apocalyptic dimension of Isaiah 65, where the wolf and lamb sit down over a shared meal. According to Brown Douglas, this is the vision that fuels black faith's moral imagination. She contends that the moral imagination, grounded in hopeful response to God's faithfulness to act, empowers "black bodies to live as free black bodies, despite the forces that would deny that fact."[35]

When we talk about radical imagination *as a component* of the preacher-as-teacher, we are talking about the capacity to envision the world differently through preaching, through the lenses of the *basileia tou Theou.* This means that we see our way past the -isms and phobias formed by the disimagination machines in our world—racism, homophobia, xenophobia, militarism, and so forth—not by any sort of Pollyannaish do-gooding, but rather with the subversive critique and hope of people who have seen God's vision for the world. The radical imagination of the preacher-as-teacher is intricately linked to a vision of the public sphere shaped by the reign of God.

Critique

The capacity for and necessity of critique grow out of this radical imagination. I have already noted the significant resonance with Brueggemann's work on prophetic imagination. He goes on to detail how "the alternative consciousness to be nurtured, on the one hand, serves to criticize in dismantling the dominant consciousness. To that extent, it attempts to do what the liberal tendency has done, engage in a rejection and delegitimizing of the present ordering of things."[36] In other words, when radical imagination takes root, it subjects the dominant powers, what Brueggemann elsewhere calls "royal consciousness," to critique and ultimate rejection.

Kenyatta Gilbert's excellent work on African American preaching during the Great Migration and civil rights movement forms an additional bridge between Brueggemann and critical pedagogy. As Gilbert identifies qualities of what he comes to call "Exodus Preaching," he locates the work of critical educator Paulo Freire as a significant point of contact. Gilbert sees similarities in the preachers of this era to Freire's educational practice of "conscientization," where people are brought to awareness of how forceful, often negative powers shape their lives in such a way that they are able to name this reality for themselves.[37] While Gilbert defines *conscientization* as "naming reality," it functions in a similar way as critique. This unmasking of forms of cultural power and oppression grant agency to preacher and listeners, setting the stage for radical imagination.

44

Preaching that engages in critique will help listeners tease out the layers of their entanglement in cultural forms of dominance and oppression. This invokes the role of critical thinking that I raised earlier. Indeed as Giroux states, "public and higher education, however deficient, were once viewed as the bedrock for educating young people to be critical and engaged citizens. . . . This meant learning how to engage in a culture of questioning, restaging power in productive ways, and connecting knowledge to the exercise of self-determination and self-development."[38] This forms the goal of critique for the preacher-as-teacher: to help raise listeners to be critical and engaged, thoroughly capable of questioning how power and knowledge are at work to limit some while others flourish. I shared above the goal from Giroux of making "despair unconvincing and hope practical." The words leading to this quote in another source, however, are what is important for us here. For Giroux, teachers *"must work to create the conditions that give students the opportunity to become citizens who have the knowledge and courage to struggle* in order to make despair unconvincing and hope practical."[39] So too with the preacher-as-teacher. In their sermons, preachers must "work to create the conditions" by which listeners can understand their lives, interpret them, then name and condemn the dominant powers that impinge upon them to work various kinds of death.

This kind of preaching is a different mode than solely declarative statements about oppressive ideologies and structures. In a shorthand explanation, there is a difference between the kind of sermon that declares "X, Y, Z are bad" and the kind of sermon that leads listeners to consider: "Let's explore together how X, Y, and Z affect our lives, our community, and our world." One poses a certain closure. The other seeks to create conditions for listeners to come to understanding and their own critique. Let me be clear: there is room for both of these. Jesus's proclamation of "Woe unto you!" is just as important, just as vital as parables about mustard seeds, lost sheep, and anything else. A monolithic form of critique does not exist for the preacher-as-teacher. But in a polarized environment, the latter will last longer than the former. What matters to the preacher-as-teacher is creating the conditions for others to first think critically about dominant ideologies and oppressive structures, then to bring them under scrutiny for how they present obstacles to imagining our way toward the realm of God.

One of the practices that Giroux advances as inherent to radical imagination, which is also implicit in bell hooks's work, is to see the work toward "an understanding of the wider relations and connections of power that young people and others can overcome uniformed practice, isolated struggles, and modes of singular politics that become insulated and self-sabotaging."[40] Giroux advocates teaching students the critical capacity to move beyond the focus on single issues in order to see their historical roots and the ways one political, economic, and cultural issue is related to another, so as to connect multiple issues together and "build a united front in the call for a radical democracy."[41]

For instance, predominantly white communities of faith perhaps need this work more than others, as they exist within layers of often unrecognized privilege, benefiting from whiteness and cultural racism that are deeply connected to economic and political privilege. Criticism of privilege may result in resistance from listeners. As the old accusation against the preacher goes, "You've gone from preaching to meddling!" Of course, these kind of responses are to be expected. Still for others, they may experience something like scales falling from their eyes. "I've never thought about my life in that way before," we might hear in the handshake line out the door. When we work to create conditions where others can exercise their own critical thinking through our preaching, and draw conclusions together about how to proceed, we allow them to see and question how their lives participate in dominant and oppressive powers. This participatory, collaborative, empowering ethic lies at the heart of what we might also call "resistance preaching." At its best, preaching will enable others to name and live their own criticisms of the way things are. This is the agency about which Giroux, Freire, and hooks believe must be active in students; it is the kind of faith that speaks back to and works against the "disimagination machine."

Possibility/Hope

On the other side of criticism is recognizing possibility and instilling hope. To return to Brueggemann, after he outlines criticism as a component of dismantling royal consciousness, he adds that "the alternative consciousness to be nurtured serves to energize persons and communities by its promise of another time and situation toward which the community of faith may move. To that extent it attempts to do what the conservative tendency has done, to live in fervent anticipation of the newness that God has promised and will surely give."[42] The flip side of criticism becomes energizing people through the promise of God's faithfulness throughout time.

Otis Moss III has identified this hope-filled proclamation as the "gospel shout" moment in the rhythm of what he calls "Blue Note Preaching."[43] Moss identifies James Weldon Johnson's *God's Trombones*, seeing in that work "the preacher's role to create a new world with words, tones, dynamics, and a Blues sensibility. The artistic construction inherent in the sermon and the collective consciousness of the people create a healing moment to reconnect the fractured personality of a community traumatized by the institution of human trafficking known as slavery."[44] Notice what Moss calls this: "a healing moment" that is able to carry the traumatized listeners forward into hopeful moments where identity might be reconfigured.

The preacher-as-teacher speaks with anticipation of what might come when radical imagination takes root and begins to blossom in the community. Kelly Brown Douglas articulates this context of hope by locating it in the apocalyptic vision of Isaiah 65 and in the speech of Martin Luther King Jr. This is also the apocalyptic vision of Revelation as Brian Blount sees it. In reviewing the claims of Revelation 6:9-11 and 20:4, Blount notes that "by this witness to Jesus' lordship, the same truth to which Jesus himself witnessed, they helped drive Satan out of heaven. This is an astounding claim. Yet it is the cosmic truth upon which they can depend and have hope. They know now what their witness can do. If their witness helped bring down Satan, surely it can help overturn the claims of historical leadership made by Rome."[45] He continues by talking about black preachers who connect God's coming justice with the struggles of the American past that resulted in moving toward equality. As he notes, "the realization of what did happen gives hope and assurance that full equality one day will happen."[46] This is the hope-filled proleptic living Kelly Brown Douglas describes, and which the preacher-as-teacher informed by critical pedagogy will enact. Critique without possibility/hope leads to despair rather than resistance to the "disimagination machine." Brueggemann, Gilbert, Brown Douglas, and Blount point us in the direction of historically informed, apocalyptically grounded possibility/hope as constituent of the radical imagination.

Critique, Possibility/Hope, and Radical Imagination Come Together

So, preaching becomes more than "preaching the text" or "preaching the Bible." That is perhaps the greatest task-oriented pitfall of the current configuration of the preacher-as-teacher. The preacher-as-teacher does not simply point to God's faithfulness in the past, building a bridge to the contemporary. Instead, preaching becomes proclamation of the possibilities for the public sphere inherent to the radical imagination shaped by the realm of God. Critique points to the faithless dead-ends in our world while also pointing to the fresh possibilities that may emerge. Here I admit a bit of a love-hate relationship with some things Paul Scott Wilson has said about the relationship between teaching and preaching.

In his book *Setting Words on Fire*, Wilson makes important observations about how teaching is a necessary function of preaching. Wilson notes that teaching "provides information that listeners can use to shape their thoughts and actions. Teaching gives people ways to think about the faith, God, and daily life. Teaching may even be said to generate consciousness by naming things we have not noticed, thereby opening them to experience.... Teaching... leads people toward faith and sets certain tasks before them that help appropriate the teachings for their lives."[47] Throughout this book, I have been working to fill out the dimensions of what constitutes teaching, hopefully giving a different sense to the limited feature Wilson names. But Wilson contends that there is still a sharp difference between teaching and *proclamation*.

For Wilson, teaching always functions in service to proclamation, never able to fulfill this greater function that he seeks to draw out of preachers. For Wilson, proclamation

> introduces people to God. They hear God speak. When preaching stops short of proclamation, arguably its main purpose is lost. Proclamation at its best is the loving announcement of the good news that has been accomplished in Jesus Christ, the articulation of words at the heart of the gospel that are spoken or received as being directly from God to the people of God. Proclamation is passionate, often almost musical speech that is intimate, urgent, and inspires confidence and faith. It actualizes the biblical text, brings the gospel to life, performs God's grace, and enacts God's liberation in the moment such that listeners experience that redemption is theirs in this present moment.[48]

Later on, he laments that sermons are filled with good subjects constitutive of this teaching function: "biblical interpretation; theological reflection; historical, cultural, and social analysis; ethical inquiry and discernment; as well as matters of social outreach and pastoral care."[49] In part, I think Wilson is right. In this heartfelt text he names what he believes is the missing component of a declining church that has failed to capture the hearts of people. He deeply wants something more from preaching, something worthy of the gospel to which it is called. And he soars with this theological description of proclamation because he believes that preachers have lost focus on God and the gospel in service of many other lesser homiletic tasks. But while I laud Wilson for wanting more out of preaching than a "bus tour to some royal estate," I believe he creates an unnecessary distinction between teaching and proclamation, even as he admits a porous boundary between the two.[50] Indeed, I have tried to make the case that the preacher-as-teacher announces and testifies to the significance of God's realm made known in Jesus Christ as a proleptic reality through radical imagination. Done with radical imagination as an indispensable, nurturing partner for one's preaching ministry, I believe the preacher-as-teacher accomplishes the tasks that Wilson defines as proclamation.

To engage in what is assuredly a reductionistic, hyperbolic characterization, the solution to the problem Wilson describes is not to simply say "God" louder in our preaching with the hopes that God will show up. The problem for Wilson is a kind of God-absence in preaching. What I am increasingly worried about is that our preaching, situated within the church's broader ministries, approximates something akin to a "dead zone of the imagination." Not that our preaching isn't creative. On the contrary, now more than ever a great many resources exist to help us craft lively sermons that use the greatest of our creative faculties with creative sermon forms, language and story, and the character of narrative dimension and poetic depth. To be fair, Wilson points to this, but defaults to calling the problem "teaching." Instead, I want to appropriate Giroux, who says, "Like the dead space of the American mall, the school systems promoted by the un-reformers offer the empty ideological seduction of consumerism as the ultimate form of citizenship and learning."[51] Can you hear resonances of the American church in this comparison? Enabled by the preaching that forms the church's weekly core rhetoric about who it is, what it values, and where it is headed, the church more and more resembles the American mall, where the satisfaction and satiation of the individual triumphs. The personal soul and its condition is what matters, and the church's ministries, chief among them the ministry of the word, has in many cases become small, no longer casting a vision of God's own radical imagination for the world, or lifting up the places in the world where the seeds for that radical imagination are taking root.

Recently I was invited to preach at a local church that uses the Narrative Lectionary. So in the third week of Lent the text given to me was John 18:12-27. In this passage, Jesus comes before Annas and the Jewish authorities for questioning; and when he responds, one of the guards assaults him. Meanwhile, Peter waits outside the gate and denies Jesus. This preaching invitation came just a few weeks after the massacre at Marjory Stoneman Douglas High School in Parkland, Florida, and the subsequent protests against gun violence by students at that school and across the nation. From the murders of Trayvon Martin and Michael Brown to the mass shootings at movie theatres, concert venues, and schools across the country, the students have responded to these situations by simply speaking the truth. In response, in print, video, and social media, adults have vilified them, even threatening them with violence. The National Rifle Association went on a media blitz to nullify them.

In terms of creative juxtaposition and association, I cannot read Jesus in this passage without seeing these young people speaking truth about the situations that have brought them and their communities into the public eye. They refuse to be moved from their mission of imagining a world where young people live without threat of violence from those who are armed with military-style weapons or from military-clad civic authorities. I see in them a likeness to the radical imagination of Jesus, who refused to move from his adherence to the kingdom of God he proclaimed in word and in deed. But I must also admit to succumbing to Peter's temptation, sitting at the edge of their story, distancing myself from their resolute action. Or perhaps worse, like Annas, and like many contemporary religious authorities (self-styled or otherwise) have done recently in their preaching, I am tempted to consolidate what power I have in favor of a smaller imagination of God's vision for the world. In short, I critique myself and other adults like me in this imaginative work, but I hold out the possibility that like them, we might have the resolve to live into (and preach) the radical imagination Jesus took to the cross and beyond. This sermon is included in chapter 5.

Some questions for the preacher-as-teacher to explore when planning sermons:

1. Does this sermon simply *condemn* as a form of critique or does this sermon *create* the conditions for listeners to have the knowledge and courage to struggle toward responsible critique? What is most appropriate for this sermon?

2. How does this sermon help listeners not just *identify* but *live with* hope?

3. What realities work to form the "disimagination machine" in the public sphere of which we are part?

4. How might this sermon foster our radical imagination? And what is the content created by that imagination?

5. How does this sermon and the liturgy around it form opportunities for people to use their agency to embody that radical imagination?

Chapter Four

Redefining Church as Classroom

Authority, the Congregation, and the "Teaching Sermon"

... being a teacher is being with people.[1]
—Ron Sapp

Just who is this preacher-as-teacher? Beyond the broader concepts and ideas I have raised previously, what kinds of practices does the preacher-as-teacher take up? How does she move within the community and negotiate her authority and relationship with the community as the one who rises to speak week in and week out? As I've argued, the preacher-as-teacher does not participate in an arcane definition of teaching as it relates to authority. The preacher-as-teacher is not the all-knowing figure who transfers theological content or skills. He or she is not the sage-on-the-stage. Furthermore, as I've pointed out, the image of the "prophetic preacher" is difficult to sustain throughout one's ministry. But I also think part of the difficulty of the image of the prophetic preacher relates to widely held notions of authority, leadership, and relationship. I do not believe this is the case with the preacher-as-teacher. Although I have already named some larger frames for understanding preaching-as-teaching, in this chapter I want to outline some characteristics of the ethos of the preacher-as-teacher as it relates to authority, to the congregation, and a revised understanding of the "teaching sermon," with some possibilities as to how one might preach this kind of teaching sermon.

Questions of Authority

As I write, public school teachers in West Virginia have successfully finished their strike while educators in Oklahoma continue to strike, and those in Kentucky are at odds with their lawmakers over classroom funding and teacher pay. There is no question that teaching as a profession is undergoing a significantly diminished sense of authority, both culturally and institutionally. Public school teachers are subject to less autonomy over the shape and content of their classrooms. The rise of standardized testing, uniform educational standards, merit pay, and other bureaucratic initiatives at federal and state levels mean that teaching is rapidly becoming divorced from the contextual realities of everyday life for many students (particularly poor and non-white students). Teachers feel the pressures to "teach to the test" and to cover required curricular materials handed down from above. The emergence of charter schools highlights the ways corporate interests have now begun to shape educational endeavors. Teachers' authority to shape teaching and learning according to the needs and experiences in each individual classroom has diminished.

And while the preacher's authority may not be diminishing in terms of autonomy to establish the shape and content of preaching in parallel fashion, preaching has experienced a diminished sense of authority in ecclesial and cultural realms. Preaching bases its authority, at least in part, on the gathered community that grants authority to the preacher, that invites the preacher to perform regular interventions into its life together for the purposes of articulating a shared ecclesial imagination, and that shares the resources for the good of life together. But that granted authority is receding in many ways. So, tradition, church, and culture have set a choice before preachers: we can conceive of our authority in an alternative mode or we can reclaim authority through authoritarian speech practices.

Without doubt, we live in a time of resurging authoritarian types of speech. The rise of the forty-fifth president has put this on full display. Individuals find themselves increasingly isolated from one another through technological influence, while news media mediates these authoritarian voices to us filtered through neoliberal capitalistic influences. Indeed, we live in an era where "fake news" is decried from one corner or another, from one end of the political spectrum to another. These deep suspicions affect our relationships with one another, and in the fissures authoritarian speech rises to ostensibly point us in the direction of "truth." The church and the ministry of preaching are not immune from these dangers. We do not have to look far to see how religious power seeks to collude with political power to form some unholy and destructive alliances. All of this has potential to work its way into the pulpit.

We need to highlight one specific danger preachers face in the effort to stand in the prophets' shoes. The counter-witness of the prophetic preacher can potentially get caught up in the same forms of authoritarian types of speech as those with ill-intent. Even prophets can sound authoritarian. Critical theorist Theodor Adorno pointed to the dangers of how Christian preachers might fall into the trappings of authoritarian speech in his analysis of the 1930s US radio preacher Martin Luther Thomas.[2] Adorno identified Thomas's use of rhetorical and ideological tools such as presenting himself as "the lone wolf," who "play[s] up one's own courage and integrity in order to win the confidence of those who feel that they are underdogs and alone," which leads to manipulation.[3] Other devices include modeling "emotional release" and excess in speech; championing the speaker's own tirelessness amidst a heavy workload for the cause; and communicating that they are "not the savior, but only his messenger," which covers a thinly veiled "ironic humility."[4] There are additional marks, but it is important here to simply say that these are points along the way where the prophet-preacher might get caught up in these types of devices just as easily as the authoritarian demagogue.

I am suggesting that it is entirely possible that the prophet can use the same speech tools of authoritarianism, even when a faith leader exists in a positive relationship with his or her community, and even with a benevolent message consonant with the radical imagination of the kingdom of God. And in a situation where the mainline church's numbers, respectability, and cultural power are diminishing, we do well to be especially cautious of the danger this presents. In attempting to speak truth to power, we may very well succumb to the problem of authoritarian speech and worse, authoritarian relationships with listeners, in what we deem prophetic preaching. This relationship can even be welcomed by listeners who long for certainty and strong leadership.

Additionally, I am concerned that the value we place on being a prophetic preacher places tremendous pressure to be a charismatic leader within the community. Kyle Brooks has written helpfully about this with respect to African American religious leadership wherein the "ratification [of black public religious leadership] plays out within a layered context defined by a black public sphere wherein rhetoric, ethos, and image co-construct the model of an idealized, charismatic black religious leader."[5] I contend that in many aspects Brooks's description reaches beyond the boundaries of race, such that leaders like Martin Luther King Jr. (historical) and William J.

Barber II (contemporary) provide types of charismatic leadership that are highly influential beyond boundaries of race and gender. In fact, when I show clips of preaching that move just as easily between the boundaries of church and into the public sphere for majority white students, I am drawn to charismatic speakers like King and Barber. But in some respects, this is to these students' detriment! The fact is that not all preachers will inhabit the charismatic leader type. And yet, they will have significant things to say without being effusive, attractional, verbal artists, and without having a dynamism that commands attention in ways that we've been socialized to associate with modern-day prophets.[6]

Continuing to build on the problems with the prophet image I have identified, reinforcing one's identity as a prophet does little to reorder relationships in the community. The danger of the preacher-as-prophet is that she still stands apart from the community, even oppositional in some ways (depending on the community), privileged to the vision that God has shared with him, and often even immune to the conditions that affect the people. But this does not have to be so. The preacher-as-teacher through the lens of critical pedagogy imagines authority and relationship differently.

Reordered relationships are at the forefront of, and even inherent to, how the preacher relates to the community. In describing how an increasing awareness of class changed her own teaching, bell hooks states, "there can be no intervention that challenges the status quo if we are not willing to interrogate the way our presentation of self as well as our pedagogical process is often shaped by middle-class norms.... This has helped me to employ pedagogical strategies that create ruptures in the established order, that promote modes of learning which challenge bourgeois hegemony."[7] Identifying class as a major component of her own identity as a teacher, in addition to race and gender, allowed hooks to move toward the kind of "interventions" (by which she means teaching moments and strategies) that challenge the dominant ordering of relationships. In other words, hooks recognized that it was not just altering the content of her teaching that would bring change, but rather a reassessment of how she viewed and presented herself as a teacher in relationship to her students. So for hooks, "the classroom becomes a dynamic place where transformations in social relations are concretely actualized."[8] More specifically, Henry Giroux makes clear that in this kind of educational ethos, "such a pedagogy listens to students, gives them a voice and role in their own learning, and recognizes that teachers not only educate students but also learn from them."[9]

This re-envisioning of authority and relationship with students prompts those of us who preach to think about two essential features of our preaching ministry: (1) what might we say of the authority of the preacher-as-teacher and (2) what does the role of the preacher-as-teacher mean for the relationship between preacher and listeners? In some sense, these questions have been at the forefront of homiletic thought in the last generation. With the breakdown in traditional notions of authority, scholars of preaching have tried to reimagine the preacher's sense of authority. Thus, Fred Craddock's seminal *As One Without Authority* imagines the preacher designing a sermon as a journey taken together with listeners where they ultimately choose how to think and act.[10] Thomas Long's widely used introductory textbook famously talks about the preacher as one who arises from the pews as one among the congregation, sent as a witness to what she has experienced in the biblical text.[11] In relation to this, homiletic scholarship has tried to think about the ethics of preaching (in distinction to ethics *in* preaching), which naturally includes analysis and prescriptions for conceiving the preacher's authority and relationship to listeners. In what follows I define some of the qualities of the teaching sermon that continue to build on the ideas of critical pedagogy as they refine an understanding of the ethics of the preacher with special attention to authority and relationship to the listening congregation. The preacher-as-teacher can cultivate these qualities in their preaching.

The Teaching Sermon Is Conversational

Often when the word *conversation* in relation to preaching comes up, many automatically think about the preacher's style, or a function of the preacher's self-presentation and presence. The preacher seems approachable, relatable, "down to earth," and as if he or she is "talking with" listeners, as opposed to talking down to them. But the past generation of homiletic thought has helped us think about conversation not necessarily as a style of delivery but rather as a kind of embodiment of authority. The idea of preaching as conversation informs our conception of the preacher-as-teacher. In much of what we have seen, critical pedagogy does not believe teaching to be a mono-directional speech or transfer of content. This is at the core foundation of Paulo Freire's thought. For Freire, the teacher "is not afraid to meet the people or to enter into dialogue with them. This person does not consider himself or herself the proprietor of history or of all people, or the liberator of the oppressed; but he or she does commit himself or herself, within history, to fight at their side."[12] Freire reorients the relationship of the teacher to students, acknowledging that dialogue becomes revelatory on the way toward mutual liberation.

The same sense of the preacher's power and relationship to the congregation has been present in the work of John McClure, first in his book *The Roundtable Pulpit*, later in *Other-wise Preaching*, and then in other important essays where he images the preacher as "guest-host" and as a leader of conversation.[13] Similarly, Lucy Rose's book *Sharing the Word*, O. Wesley Allen's *The Homiletic of All Believers*, as well as Ronald Allen and O. Wesley Allen's *The Sermon Without End* have all been formative expressions for thinking about preaching as "conversation."[14] Broadly speaking, these works have scrutinized traditional givens of the preacher's authority, proposing that those who do not preach become (to one degree or another) participants in the ongoing work of proclamation as biblical texts come into "conversation" with life and culture and the desire to live as the people of God. The authority of the preacher is less hierarchical, less dependent on institutional foundations, and more grounded in relational and experiential types of authority, where meaning and authority remain continually under negotiation. A kind of mutuality between preacher and listener emerges, similar to what we have seen above in the work of bell hooks. Preaching that functions within this mode of teaching will live into the kind of solidarity found in these notions of "conversation."

A newer component to the notion of conversation is that of Kwok Pui-Lan, who envisions that "the aim of postcolonial preaching is to create a multivocal and dialogical faith community committed to justice."[15] In a postcolonial world where many speak the dominant language and their mother tongue, the church's preaching cannot just be conversational, but must also be *heteroglossic*. By this she means that preaching becomes more communal and participatory and even more, preaching becomes a ground for intercultural sharing and sensitivity. Preaching becomes a kind of "third space," where the congregation "examine[s] the 'inter' in our identities, languages, and cultures, and by doing so encounter[s] the liberating grace of God in fresh ways."[16]

All of this means that we prepare for our weekly sermons differently: we listen to more voices from different places, and in listening we admit the limits of our own understanding. Our preaching becomes more conversational, not simply in a kind of rhetorical pulpit style, but in its ethos. Indeed it becomes more collaborative and, perhaps, more joyful when we have something difficult to say because our preaching comes out of a place of deep solidarity with others. The preacher-as-teacher through critical pedagogy fosters different kinds of relationships.

The Teaching Sermon Uses Border Pedagogy and Fugitive Forms of Knowledge

The preacher-as-teacher's commitment to conversational preaching changes the ethos of the preacher. One way of envisioning this is through what Giroux calls "border pedagogy," which

> both confirms and critically engages the knowledge and experience through which students author their own voices and construct social identities. This suggests taking seriously the knowledge and experiences that constitute the individual and collective voices by which students identify and give meaning to themselves and others and drawing upon what they know about their own lives as a basis for criticizing the dominant culture. In this case, student experience has to be first understood and recognized as the accumulation of collective memories and stories that provide students with a sense of familiarity, identity, and practical knowledge. Such experience has to be both affirmed and critically interrogated.[17]

For the preacher-as-teacher, this means seeking ways to be in mutuality and solidarity with listeners, attempting to understand how their faith and faith practices have been constructed, then affirming and critically interrogating them. This builds upon the kind of multidirectional and conversational mode of preaching I described above. But again, at the heart of border pedagogy that finds its way into the pulpit, the preacher-as-teacher seeks a different kind of authority and different authoritative sources. Giroux goes on to illustrate how border pedagogy "provides opportunities for teachers to deepen their own understanding of the discourse of various others in order to effect a more dialectical understanding of their own politics, values, and pedagogy."[18] In other words, for preachers this means that we might just be changed in the process of conversation—which we may very well be hesitant to do!

Part of that change means that there are revisions in what counts for preachers as valid forms of what we might call "theological knowledge." In describing classrooms where critical pedagogy operates, Giroux says, "critical pedagogical practices also allow students to produce and appropriate space for the production of fugitive knowledge forms, those forms of knowledge that exist either outside of the mainstream curriculum or are seen as unworthy of serious attention."[19] In conversational preaching, the preacher-as-teacher seeks to find, understand, and lift up "fugitive forms of knowledge" regarding faith and practice. Drawing on this concept, I make the case in my book *Youthful Preaching* that adolescent youth can provide us with such knowledge, shaping how we think about our collective Christian identity.[20] Young people have a wealth of wisdom that we often bypass because the disimagination machines in our culture render young people lifeless and useless from the neck up. Whether a preacher is seeking to interpret a scripture text or doctrine or aspect of life and culture, the preacher-as-teacher creates the spaces for others to produce their own ideas of faith and seeks out "fugitive forms" of faith; while they might be seen as outside the mainstream or unworthy of attention by others, they might just inform the faith of a community of sermon listeners. This means that the preacher-as-teacher looks in unlikely places for theological knowledge, forms "fugitive" relationships with people beyond the boundaries of acceptable faith and practice, and as Anna Carter Florence describes, even "dislocates" exegesis of texts by reading and interpreting in unlikely places, in unlikely ways, and with previously unlikely people.[21] Fugitive forms of knowledge are rarely found in commentaries, as helpful as they can be. In seeking to teach, the preacher-as-teacher attempts to discover what listeners bring to the table as helpful to the ongoing life of being the community of faith together.

This way of envisioning the preacher-as-teacher dovetails with current discussions of conversation and authority already at work in the literature about preaching. But they are not far from the same types of discussion also at work in critical pedagogy (not coincidentally they are roughly concurrent).

The Teaching Sermon Is "Friendly" and "Frank"

How does the relationship of the preacher-as-teacher with the congregation change? What does the teaching sermon sound like? It might strike us rather odd at first glance to consider the sermon as an exercise of friendship, especially as a component of the teaching sermon. We often hold commonplace assumptions about friendship that mean equality, emotional closeness, and intimate exchange. And these qualities describe what we tend to value in friendship. But rarely do these qualities define the relationship between teacher and student. Some of the teachers from whom I learned the most never approached me as though I was a student with little to offer in return. High school teachers like Mrs. Scott who taught civics and sociology, Mr. Zappia who taught math (ugh!), and Mrs. Cooper who taught language arts and newspaper were pivotal people in my journey. Undoubtedly they functioned as people who conveyed important information, but they also cultivated healthy personal relationships with me and other students by creating an atmosphere that reached beyond transactional teaching and learning. They believed students had something significant to offer to the learning experience. Educator Hannah Spector imagines a classroom where friendship is a goal, except that "friendship is not about acquiring friends on Facebook or followers on Twitter. Rather, it is about having youth that can learn about their neighbors, where similarities and differences are discovered, and where common ground can be achieved in the hopes of building little worlds of solidarity. These little worlds can pave the way to developing communities beyond classrooms, too."[22] When I raise the idea of the preacher-as-teacher as friend, we might think of this nature of friendship as a key to what I mean: building little worlds of solidarity over ordered hierarchy. And while this characterization should be true, the preaching and ministry of Jesus strengthens how we might think of preaching as friendship.

Gail O'Day examines friendship in the Greco-Roman context, connecting the depiction of Jesus in the Gospel of John to a way of thinking about preaching as friendship. As O'Day begins to frame her study, she recounts that "in the ancient world, friendship was equally about what and how one speaks."[23] O'Day claims that there is something about the rhetorical act that can condition our concept of friendship. Such rhetorical marks of friendship were described in the ancient world through people like Socrates, Plutarch, and Cicero as *parrēsia*, which translates to "frank speech" or "plain speaking."[24] O'Day outlines three important contexts in which friendship and frankness of speech were especially significant: (1) patron-client relationships, where the patron needed to discern if relationships were engaged in flattery to improve their standing; (2) philosophical schools, in which instruction was best characterized by frank speech; and (3) the context of philosophical debates, in which frank speech allowed "freedom of speech and could involve taking unpopular or risky positions for the sake of intellectual honesty and truth."[25]

O'Day sets the first and second contexts for *parrēsia* against Jesus's conversation with his disciples in John's farewell discourse, specifically John 16:25-32 where Jesus informs the disciples, "I've been using figures of speech with you. The time is coming when I will no longer speak to you in such analogies. Instead, I will tell you plainly about the Father." In John, Jesus exemplifies plain speech, the language of true friendship. This kind of plain speaking allows the disciples to experience for themselves the kind of intimate relationship Jesus described having with "the Father." Indeed, "everything I heard from my Father I have made known to you" (John 15:15), which is linked directly to the language of friendship as defining the relationship between Jesus and the disciples. This has a kind of transitive effect, where "Jesus' plain speaking, through which he treats the disciples as peers and not as servants, equips them to lead a life of love and friendship themselves."[26] Plain speaking opens the path to friendship, which in turn empowers the disciples to live as followers of the way of Jesus. Because Jesus shares what God first shared with him through plain speech, the disciples are enabled to live in and act with love, justice, and mercy.

O'Day then moves to describe that for contemporary preaching, this does not equate to "be[ing] friendly" in preaching, for "there is plenty of friendliness in much of the church's preaching—jokes, chatter, anecdotes told simply to make a congregation smile or to get them on one's good side, tangential personal asides—but friendliness is not the same thing as gospel friendship."[27] Instead, O'Day means to say that preachers should engage in plain speech that reorders relationships with listeners. But this is also the kind of speech in which Jesus engages before the high priest, the third context of *parrēsia*. This is truth-telling: "bold, frank, open speech, a speech that is measured and assessed by its enactment of love, not its demonstration of power...always reciprocal, always contain[ing] within it the invitation to friendship for those who hear."[28] Cornel West furthers the case for this third context of *parrēsia* as a practice capable of renewing the public sphere. Speaking of Socrates' use of plain speech as a way "to unleash painful wisdom seeking—his midwifery of ideas and visions—was predicated on the capacity of all people...to engage in a critique of and resistance to the corruptions of mind, soul, and society."[29] West continues by describing this as a sustaining practice for democratic energy, capable of infusing democratic practice with what we have called the radical imagination. But I urge a caution in this connection to preaching, which most preachers will recognize as a danger of prophetic preaching: "fearless speech" that "unsettles, unnerves, and unhouses people from their uncritical sleepwalking" never comes as uncalculated, reckless, divisive, or loveless speech that serves our own power or disregards the agency of listeners.[30] Our preaching always comes in service of the way of love shaped by the *basileia tou Theou*.

In preaching toward a vision of the public sphere characterized by the kingdom of God, our kingdom-talk is known by the rhetorical practice of Jesus: friendly and frank, rooted in love. In essence, reordered relationships in the kingdom of God are empowered by the plain-speech practices like those of Jesus. As those of us who have preached week to week in these contentious times know, this is not always easy! This is where the connection to Jesus and our connection to critical pedagogy becomes especially important. The disposition of the teacher in those most beloved of memories like I outline above are characterized by frank speech empowered by love. The preacher-as-teacher does not simply speak by dispensing knowledge that she knows will benefit others because she has the authority to do so. Rather, the teacher engages in plain speech *out of a place of deep love* and, dare I say, *passion for the things of the kingdom of God.* And people know the difference.

To picture this deep love as a function of teaching, bell hooks tells the story of a student who loved to dance. One week the student came in late to class, danced to the front, picked hooks up, and spun her around. While many might have taken this for impropriety, hooks read this as an apology for being late and as a sign of the presence of *eros* in her classroom. As a teacher, hooks seeks to cultivate love. And of this interaction in particular, she observes, "When *eros* is present in the classroom setting, then love is bound to flourish. Well-learned distinctions between public and private make us believe that love has no place in the classroom. Even though many viewers could applaud a movie like *Dead Poets Society*, possibly identifying with the passion of the professor and his students, rarely is such passion institutionally affirmed."[31] Undoubtedly, her eros-shaped interactions with this student mean that she could speak plainly with him, perhaps even about his tardiness to class. This is the connection for the preacher-as-teacher: the preacher-as-teacher passionately loves enough to speak plainly with listeners in the pulpit. This is not harsh speech. But when the sermon engages a difficult topic, listeners listen because they know they are loved; and even more, they know this frank speech signifies that love.

All of this frames why I hesitate in assigning preaching about difficult issues to the realm of the "prophetic," as has been our tendency over many years. One of the fears of speaking a prophetic word is being perceived as standing "over against" listeners and that the prophetic preacher will speak as a domineering authority, rather than as a friend. The preacher-as-teacher, however, exists in a different type of relationship. While frank speech may come as a difficult practice to cultivate, love conditions the speaking. These are extensions of imitating Jesus. The preacher-as-teacher speaks like Jesus: frank and friendly.

The Teaching Sermon Is
Embodied in Action

Up to this point, I have not mentioned the designation of Jesus as "teacher." But this title clearly functions as an important identifier for Jesus in the Gospels. In fact, according to Brian Blount, the characters in the Gospel of Mark prefer this title for Jesus. But much to our surprise, "though the Markan Jesus is clearly understood to be a teacher, he is rarely seen teaching any particular content. Rather, he teaches performatively. His actions and words intend more than the conveyance of information."[32] As Blount reads Jesus in the Gospel of Mark, Jesus's teaching reaches beyond the bounds of words and ideas to the realm of performance and action. Not unlike what I have described of critical pedagogy throughout this book, Jesus's teaching does not just seek to download information about the kingdom of God to those who will carry on his ministry. From this perspective, we might call this depiction the "Freirean Jesus" or "Jesus, the critical pedagogue." But an important clarifier is warranted here before unpacking the categories Blount provides. Jesus's speaking and action placed him in the path of an almost certain death. So we will have to be careful of using Jesus as a model for the preacher-as-teacher. If Jesus functions as a model for the preacher-as-teacher, it can only be in a modified, limited form. Contemporary pastors occupy a different role than Jesus and thus will speak and act differently than Jesus did.

Blount identifies four categories by which Jesus's teaching goes beyond simple, traditional notions of teaching. And while Blount's categories are focused toward what we call Christian education, as we have come to discover, the lines between teaching and preaching are more blurry than we might have thought before.

1. Jesus teaches by enacting the reign of God.

By this, Blount means that Jesus's life becomes a living pointer to the "Reign of God." Jesus did not live his life in such a way that he pointed to himself, but rather to the life-giving reality of God's realm. So "if we want to teach the Reign of God, we start by finding a way to live the Reign of God, as Jesus lived it, by crafting a curriculum that not only conveys information about the Reign, but, more importantly, shapes the very reality the Reign intends to convey."[33] From the Gospel of Mark, Jesus heals beyond socially accepted barriers that created insiders and outsiders. For Jesus, the kingdom of God is not bound by social barriers or even by religious codes about purity and impurity, but rather by the pursuit of *shalom* healing and wholeness that ends up exposing those boundaries as false. Jesus teaches by way of living out what he spoke and speaking about what he lived.

2. Jesus teaches by engaging hopelessness.

Blount identifies a literary marker in the times that Jesus is addressed as "Teacher" in the Gospel of Mark. In each of these instances, the situation is one of presumed hopelessness. Blount references them all: the disciples in the boat caught in a storm, a man whose child has been possessed by a demon since birth, an unknown character the disciples have seen healing in Jesus's name, the question about inheriting eternal life, James and John's argument over seating arrangements in the fulfillment of all things, the verbal traps of the religious leaders, the disciples marveling at the stones of the temple that have a doomed destiny, and the request for the upper room. In all of these places, hopelessness rises. And in each instance of hopelessness, Jesus speaks or acts in ways that bring healing, or at least the possibility of healing.

3. Jesus teaches by crossing boundaries.

Blount points us to Mark 4:35 to show us how Jesus crosses ethnic boundaries as he physically crosses "to the other side" in the boat with the disciples, whereupon stepping out of the boat at the beginning of Mark 5 Jesus encounters the (Gentile!) Gerasene demoniac. This crossing leads to healing. And this dual crossing composes another component of Jesus's "teaching—that is, acting, living with authority and power that no teacher any of [the disciples] had known had ever displayed before."[34]

4. Jesus's teaching meets resistance.

In this final category, Blount points to the various forces that compose resistance to the authority of Jesus and, more specifically, to the reign of God that seeks to break down boundaries. In Blount's examination of Mark 4:35-41, these include demonic forces and nature in the form of wind and waves. But we might think even more expansively about the kinds of resistance Jesus faces: scarcity in the form of hunger, disease, and exclusion; religious and political collusion that opposes the way of shalom his ministry brings; a violent state execution in his crucifixion; and finally, death itself. The resistances are not only met by an exorcism and by calming the sea but also by healing, feeding, community-building inclusion, and the ultimate display of meeting resistance: God's power that resurrected Jesus from the power of death. Blount notes a twofold lesson for those who seek to teach in the way of Jesus: (1) there will be resistance to the teaching of the reign of God and (2) ultimately, no matter the resistance raised, humanity will be able to receive the message of the reign of God by God's power.

The idea in these four categories is simple enough, but not insignificant. Teaching is never divorced from praxis, from concrete action in the world. As critical pedagogy makes clear, pedagogical practices informed by critical theory always participate in and leads to emancipatory practice that promotes freedom and alleviates suffering.[35] Theory informs teaching that leads to practices of freedom. But Blount's insightful, descriptive framework of Jesus as teacher still leaves us at a bit of a loss for our preaching-as-teaching. Preaching that rightly participates in the kingdom of God not only imitates the ways Jesus spoke ("plain speech") but also always embodies the kingdom of God in and beyond the preaching moment. But how do *we* do that? We know that when our preaching becomes merely words without corresponding embodied action, our preaching fails the test of the vision of the public sphere found in the kingdom of God. So the teaching sermon can never stand alone as a kind of one-off, independent theological rhetorical event (teaching as information!). Participating in the vision for the new public sphere shaped by the kingdom of God, the teaching sermon becomes embodied by preacher and congregation.

This move toward embodiment involves a number of things both within the sermon and beyond it. It means that we are never satisfied with sermons that settle for abstraction. Our vision and our sermonic claims must always become concrete and within the realm of serious possibility for our listeners. The move toward embodiment means we pay attention to community and world. We never allow ourselves to fall into the trap of believing that our preaching cannot or should not address "current events." It means that we call people to wholehearted, full-throated participation in the *basileia tou Theou* in ways both big and small. And it means that we invite them to a performative, participatory kind of hope, holding out a path to live into God's vision for the world but also allowing room for God's eschatological completion. And as we do that, we do not manipulatively induce guilt for privileged listeners but paint an inspiring, (and again) concrete path toward restoration. In connecting the sermon to our liturgy and our broader church ministries, we show people how to cross boundaries and overcome resistance in the way of resurrection. And we never allow our preaching ministries to become divorced from other ministerial acts, including community organizing, advocacy, and witness for social justice, acts of mercy, pastoral care, acts of healing, and so on.

The Teaching Sermon Attends to Form

By way of concluding this chapter, I offer a brief sketch of a sermon form for the preacher-as-teacher through critical pedagogy. An annotated possibility of a sermon form serves to flesh out the pulpit practice of the preacher-as-teacher. In addition, this possible sermon form begins to tie together the different components of the preacher-as-teacher that I have articulated throughout the book. In the final bullet point under each sermon move, I also return in brief to the sermon on gun violence I describe in the introduction. Remember that I admitted the sermon was not constructed as well as it could have been. Below I provide a framework for how this sermon might have progressed if I had approached it better.

Move 1: What kind of world is imagined and inhabited by this difficult text, subject, issue, or taboo?

In this move, the preacher breaks silences around a taboo, a difficult subject, or a difficult biblical text, drawing out the conditions that help those silences exist and the implications of a world where we are held under the silence of a taboo or difficult subject or text.

Stories about gun violence stream across our lives. But we are often silent in the church about gun violence. What keeps us silent? That we can have a very public conversation about guns—but not in the church—prompts hard questions about who benefits from silence and the kind of world where the church's silence continues.

Move 2: Critique

Using biblical, theological, and experiential resources, the preacher explains how the taboo under examination (or silence around it) works toward oppression and suffering.

The text for that Sunday was 2 Samuel 11:1-15; the story of David, Uriah, and Bathsheba. David's story warns us what happens when an abundance of power meets desire and renders a human being into an object. The church has long made this story about adultery, when it reveals just as much (if not more) about power and dehumanization. Does our culture of guns provoke us to the same dynamic, allowing our power and fear to dehumanize others?

Move 3: What kind of world is imagined if the taboo is subject to the basileia tou Theou?

The preacher employs a vision of the *basileia tou Theou* to begin imagining a new public sphere.

The *basileia tou Theou* operates under different principles than David's reign. All people are members of the community created by God. When our power and fear lead us to a gun culture, we find ourselves at odds with the principles of the *basileia tou Theou*. The realm of God imagines others not as objects to fear or overcome, but as kindred created in the image of that same loving God. Living into the *basileia tou Theou* realizes a new public sphere that casts out fear and dehumanization of one another.

Move 4: Possibility/Hope

The preacher offers the new public sphere as a world of hope and possibility, tracing out the good news to be celebrated (à la Frank Thomas[36]) and anticipating the consequences for how we live (à la Eugene Lowry[37]).

With joy, we celebrate and receive our interconnectedness in the larger human family constituted by God. But we recognize that this has implications for how we use our power to buy and use guns. We also realize that this vision calls us to use our voices to influence gun legislation and how we live within the socio-political structures of our communities. The Christian community envisions a world where none are threatened or seen as less than human, and we seize the opportunity to bear that out in our world.

I do not believe this sermon form to be original to me; in fact, in many ways it bears resemblance to what Paul Scott Wilson calls the "four pages of the sermon."[38] Nor is this sermon form exhaustive; as with the "four page sermon," I believe the work of the preacher-as-teacher can come to bear in multiple sermon forms. It is simply up to the preacher to do the work of finding the modes of preaching consistent with what I have described throughout the book as the preacher-as-teacher.

In this chapter, I have described how the preacher-as-teacher approaches authority and a relationship with the congregation in some renewed ways. Further, the teaching sermon has some particular qualities that demonstrate this kind of authority and relationship (conversation, friendship, border pedagogy or fugitive forms of knowledge, and embodied). Throughout the book, I have tried to expand our concept of the preacher-as-teacher, believing that it has much to say about preaching in our current context where so many of our listeners are weary and polarized and in which we may be burdened with juggling too many roles in our preaching ministries. In the next chapter, I offer three sermons with commentary that illustrate how the preacher-as-teacher is exemplified in the pulpit.

Chapter Five
That'll Teach

The Teaching Sermon in Action

Education is about healing and wholeness. It is about empowerment,
liberation, transcendence, about renewing the vitality of life.
It is about finding and claiming ourselves and our place in the world.[1]
—Parker Palmer

In this chapter I offer three sample sermons that characterize different
aspects of what I have described of the preacher-as-teacher through
the lens of critical pedagogy. Providing commentary on sermons in a
helpful format is notoriously difficult, so I will preface each sermon with a
brief biography of the preacher and some introductory comments about the
sermon that will characterize the larger themes of the preacher-as-teacher as
I have described in the preceding chapters. Then throughout the sermon
I will offer marginal comments that highlight specific ways in which the
sermons reflect characteristics of the teaching sermon. I will also suggest
some ways in which the sermon might have employed qualities of the teaching sermon through the lenses I have provided. This is not to suggest that
the sermons are deficient; indeed, they are very fine sermons. But I want
to highlight some possible ways that the qualities I have raised might be
incorporated into them. You might consider adding your own marginal
notes as to how these sermons function as teaching sermons through the
lens of critical pedagogy. The sermons have been edited for length and for
a written encounter.

Before we dive in, let's revisit the core themes and categories I have established through the book. Like an appendix for a textbook, I want to provide a sort of glossary for what we will look for in the sermons that follow. These terms shape our revised understanding of what we mean when we talk about preaching-as-teaching. This glossary should provide an easy reference for the sermons and comments below. Each term will have a short definition, and rather than alphabetical order, they are listed in their order of appearance in the preceding chapters.

Transformational and Public Intellectual. The preacher-as-teacher does not simply pass along biblical knowledge and theological concepts for uninformed, passive listeners, but instead seeks to use the public setting of the teaching and preaching moment for the purposes of transformation.

Interventions. The regular occasion of preaching provides interventions in the public sphere in which forms of authority, knowledge, behavior, and theological versions of life are contested. Preaching-as-teaching is an intervention in the course of life, making plain how faith speaks to the struggle and how communities of faith might navigate these contested spheres.

Critical Thinking. The preacher-as-teacher seeks to expose, examine, and help listeners assess the social, economic, political, and theological relationships that form daily life.

Transformation. Critical thought is not the end in itself. Instead, communities of faith will seek transformation that, in a Christian sense, is characterized by the biblical terms metamorphosis (transformation) and metanoia (repentance).

Public Sphere. The preacher-as-teacher accounts for preaching as a communicative event that constructs a vision for the public sphere beyond ecclesial gatherings, patterned after the *basileia tou Theou*.

Radical Imagination. The preacher-as-teacher demonstrates a capacity to envision the world (and life lived within it) differently through preaching, particularly through the lenses of the *basileia tou Theou*.

Critique. As part of the shaping of the radical imagination, the practice of critique helps listeners tease out the layers of their entanglement in cultural forms of dominance and oppression and their participation in the "disimagination machine." This invokes the task of critical thinking.

Possibility/Hope. On the other side of critique, the preacher-as-teacher speaks with anticipation of what might come when radical imagination takes root and begins to blossom in the community.

Reordered Relationships. In an age of renewed authoritarian practices and suspicion of religious leadership, the preacher-as-teacher will carefully choose new ways of preaching and being with listeners that exhibit solidarity and mutuality.

Conversational. As a component of reordered relationships, the authority of the preacher is less hierarchical, less dependent on institutional foundations, and more grounded in relational and experiential types of authority. Meaning and authority remain continually under negotiation and a kind of mutuality between preacher and listeners emerges.

Border Pedagogy and Fugitive Forms of Knowledge. An additional feature of reordered relationships, the preacher-as-teacher creates and allows spaces for others to produce their own ideas of faith and seeks forms of faith that might be seen as outside the mainstream or unworthy of attention by others, but potentially informative for the faith of a community of sermon listeners. This means that the preacher-as-teacher looks for theological knowledge in unlikely places.

Friendly. Drawing from Greco-Roman connection between friendship and speech practices, the preacher-as-teacher engages in plain speech. As such, reordered relationships in the kingdom of God are empowered by the kind of plain speech practices exhibited in the preaching of Jesus Christ. The teacher does not simply speak by dispensing knowledge that will benefit others by virtue of the preacher's authority. Rather, the preacher-as-teacher engages in plain speech out of a place of deep love for others and passion for the things of the kingdom of God.

Embodied Word. The teaching sermon can never stand alone as a kind of one-off, independent theological rhetorical event (teaching as information). Instead, patterned after Jesus the teacher, the preacher-as-teacher will perform what is spoken and invite the congregation to do the same by engaging hopelessness, crossing boundaries, and meeting resistance with the confidence of God's power.

Sermon One

Rev. Casey Thornburgh Sigmon, PhD currently serves as the minister of Weston Christian Church (Disciples of Christ) in Weston, Missouri. A graduate of the PhD program at Vanderbilt University in Homiletics and Liturgics, Casey also teaches as an adjunct in Preaching and Worship at St. Paul's School of Theology in Kansas City, Missouri. She brings a wealth of expertise to preaching and worship leadership; this sermon is no exception.

Casey begins by modeling critical thinking. She refuses the simplistic answer of mental illness, seeking to remove some of the stigma around mental illness, and replacing that simplistic answer with the theological category of anger. As important as this move is, we might want more emphasis on why mental illness doesn't suffice to explain the behavior, working to make explicit her work to remove stigma, rather than leaving it implicit. Still, this is an important intervention for a tragic situation where people surely had many questions and, perhaps, impulsive and unexamined answers to explain this behavior.

Casey's sermon, entitled "Fruit of Self-Control," was preached on November 12, 2017, for Merriam Christian Church (Disciples of Christ) in Merriam, Kansas. The biblical texts for the sermon are Galatians 5:16-26 and James 1 (especially vv. 19-25), and this was the final sermon in a series on the fruit of the Spirit. In terms of context, it was preached over Veterans Day weekend and was the first service after the shooting at First Baptist Church in Sutherland Springs, Texas. As we will see, this sermon functions as a kind of intervention to provoke the listeners' critical thinking about the theological roots of tragic actions in the world. She provides a provocative framework for the "fruit" of anger (critique) and the fruit of self-control (possibility/hope).

And in doing so she holds out the vision of a world in which the "implanted word" flowers in believers to save and keep life. The sermon imagines a public sphere in which the smallest instances of self-control have great impact in a "living network."

"Fruit of Self-Control"—Galatians 5:16-26; James 1

He had to have been angry—mind-numbingly angry to do what he did.

I suppose I cannot think of any other way to explain or justify how a human being could do what he did to walk into a church like ours filled with men and women young and old who had gathered to pray, to worship, to follow Jesus in this world. Some say he had to have been mentally ill—as if depression or anxiety could make someone explode as he did to forever alter the world—whole familiesa whole community . . . touched by his reckless behavior.

But if I could point to one rotten fruit that can grow in the hearts of humanity and lead to the violence that took place in First Baptist Church of Sutherland Springs last Sunday—and God only knows what other town in the weeks to come—I would look no further than James's letter. James has a word for us this morning, one little word with great implications: *anger.*

Linking anger to self-control, our ninth and final fruit of the Spirit in Paul's letter to the Galatians, is not so hard to do. An angry person very quickly loses control of his or her behavior. When children do it, we call it a tantrum, as an adult, a temper. It seems to me that people are growing angrier by the minute these days. And as the anger festers, it unleashes in fits of road rage and domestic violence against family members who are at an arm's length. Self-control is lost.

> Casey makes an adept pairing here of self-control with anger. This might seem like a simple move, but it helps clarify how anger manifests in ways contrary to the gospel. With regard to continuing the helpful agricultural metaphor she has started to use, I would suggest adding a couple of sentences to this paragraph like: "Anger fuses to lost self-control and we know its rotten fruit. Its stench permeates our atmosphere." In doing so, the work of critical thinking does not remain abstract but takes on the vivid language she has set up.

73

James says anger does not produce works of righteousness. Yet often, our actions out of anger create in us the illusion of self-righteousness. They had it coming, after all. Self-control gone awry is a hardness of heart that leads to numbness. Erupting angrily at the first person who gets in our way, the first person who dares to cross our path, that one person who threatens or thwarts our plan: it's self-protection at all costs. Within our angry actions lies a rottenness that corrodes from the inside of a person to the outside.

These lines suggests that Casey has been listening to her listeners and the world around her in a conversational mode, a sign of reordered relationships. It also engages hopelessness.

This is no less true when we realize that we have little control over other people and the events of this world. So it's hard some weeks not to feel discouraged. It's hard for us to feel as if there is nothing that we can do to make this world a better place, a safer place for ourselves and the ones we love.

I hear that discouragement over dinner tables and water coolers. And we can arm that fear so that we are able to meet that gnawing fear and our discouragement with the very same violence that caused it in the first place. And certainly, there are churches and schools creating measures to do just this: we arm ourselves with guns in order to feel secure.

As important as this is, and I am sure it was top of mind for many listeners, I wonder what other ways Casey might engage in critique of more everyday practices in which we "arm fear."

Or. Or we can—as crazy as it sounds—welcome with meekness the implanted word that has the power to save our souls. The implanted word, that is evidenced in our lives by the fruit that we bear—the implanted word that requires the bookends of love and self-control to nourish its growth from the inside-

Here Casey begins to introduce a world of possibility! And again she builds off the imagery she has established in the beginning of the sermon.

out. Because if all Christians really welcomed the implanted word into our actions, all of us, scattered over the world, then imagine the sort of reach our...what is it? (stretch out arms)...about three feet of individual influence could have as it meets and mingles with the living network, the living body of Christ.

Sharon Salzburg recounted for the radio program *On Being* a story of a friend's son, Frank, who tried to put this idea of simply living out kindness, gentleness, generosity, joy...you know, the fruit of the Spirit—into practice during his daily commute on the New York City subway.

Casey's example here shows how this kind of possibility is already at work in the public sphere and by someone who may or may not be part of a faith community. This could very well be a "fugitive form of knowledge."

How many of you have ever been on the NYC subway? Or the Chicago "L"? Those of you who know, public transportation is where we tend to encounter people not in their best, most Zen, self-controlled state.

It's a place where Frank often encountered people who, like him, were frazzled and quick to speak sharply, angrily, to each other. Frank often ended up responding that way too, and he wanted to stop. He wanted

The re-telling of the story from *On Being* is an effective way of making her claim concrete.

to stop spreading the things that were upsetting him to strangers who, he thought, had their own lives to worry about.

As Frank went down the stairs and through the turnstile, he thought about what he was bringing into the station with him that morning. He'd had a fight with his girlfriend, and he faced a difficult meeting when he got to work. And his back was hurting again, so his steps were jagged. Along with his anxiety about the morning news, he recognized how cranky he was. And he sensed that deep down he was looking for a fight to let some of this loose.

As it turns out, he brought with him a book he was reading, one Sharon Salzburg had written called *Lovingkindness*. There were big crowds on the platform. There had been some snafu, and three packed trains passed his station without stopping, to the jeers of the others on the platform.

Frank was angry that, through no fault of his own, he would be late to work. Finally, a train stopped. When he maneuvered through the crowd at the door, he saw it was packed with rowdy middle schoolers on a field trip. They were boisterous and physical. Naturally, he turned up the volume on his headphones to drown them out.

By using this book reference in the sermon, Casey identifies and validates this book as a fugitive form of knowledge. This is border pedagogy, as other preachers might be willing to malign a book like this as "self-help" and demur its use as an authority in relation to scripture.

At the next stop a woman holding two heavy bags in one hand and a child's hand in the other pulled the little girl through the crowd to the pole where Frank was standing. Immediately she berated him, saying he was taking up too much space, his big hand was blocking out too much of the pole, and how did he expect her little girl to get a grip? Frank wanted to bark back at her, to let anger jump out in self-defense instead of self-control.

But instead, he paused to take her in. He caught his breath. And he could see her. Likely she would be even later to work than he. She had to drop this child off at school or day care. She was literally carrying a heavy burden, two of them, and this transit situation was frustrating them all. "You know, you're right," Frank said, moving his hand higher. "Sorry about that."

One of the students careened into Frank from behind, right at the tender spot in his back. Again his first impulse was to yell at the boy, tell him to watch where he was going. Frank looked at him before he spoke and saw genuine concern in the boy's face when Frank winced from the pain in his back. "Hey, buddy, slow down," Frank told the boy with a smile. "This train is crowded." "Sorry, sorry, sorry. What's the book you're reading?" the boy asked. "It's a book about how to be kinder to each other," Frank said. "They write books about stuff like that?" the boy said, and turned back to his friends.

Think of the difference if Frank had acted on his first impulses. He'd be glowering at the woman and child, and likely the woman would be staring at him with the same fury while the child looked confused and frightened. He would have made the boy feel guilty and clumsy. Instead, the space around Frank was calmer because he'd paused rather than adding to the friction. He had done his part not to enhance the misery in the three feet around his body that were his to influence.[2]

For fruit to be real, the fruit of the Spirit—all nine of them—must be translated into deeds. Frank's deeds on the subway, and others like them, multiply calm in a world that would rather multiply anger. He will not make it in the newspaper or on Twitter for his kindness in

> The first sentence of this section that connects the story to what comes next might have been better served at the end of this paragraph, but Casey begins to imagine a world shaped by self-control that manifests itself in daily life rather than anger.

the way the shooter will, but I believe the Spirit made a difference, a different experience of the world we live in now, through him.

Gentleness, patience, goodness, all of them must be translated into deeds...and in order for us to do this work of translating the gifts of the Holy Spirit that implant in our hearts when we hear the gospel, we must always exercise self-control.

We must be disciplined. We must be persistent. For time and again, our old selves that reigned before Christ reigned in our hearts seep in. And when challenged, anger, envy, judgment, disease that infest the harvest of righteousness in our hearts and in

> Casey here is calling for transformation: *metamorphosis* and *metanoia*. However, we might invite Casey to think about the possibility of continuing to imagine what the gospel-filled world of self-control looks like in herself, in her community, and among all Christians rather than employing language like "must."

our communities choke out the fruit. They render us unrecognizable from the Savior whose name we claim for ourselves.

Do you believe it? Do you believe that God's implanted word has the power to save our lives? Not just for some far-off, out-there eternity, but now—right now—to save a life.

To stop a shooter.

> Yes! The *basileia tou Theou* takes shape here and now, not just in a world far off from here.

To stop an abuser.
To stop a bully.
To save a life?

Casey imagines how small actions ("three feet of influence") are an exercise of living by the Holy Spirit.

If you do, then will you turn in every circumstance to that word so that you can pray for the wisdom to *live* that word? The center of that three feet of influence is you. You are the one who must halt, catch your breath, that holy *ruach*, the Holy Spirit who saves us from our selfish selves.

I love this statement, as it continues to build a critique of the public sphere as-is. And it comes as a word of plain speech that also names possible resistance within ourselves. That said, it might more helpfully appear earlier in the sermon as Casey has begun to sing to us the good news of how the implanted word saves life. This turns us back to critique rather than concrete ways the possibility/hope of a life with the implanted word take shape.

Otherwise, ignoring James's offer to his community, you should abandon meekness and humility to join the ranks of the angry who gain security for themselves at the expense of any who are in their way. It's an ever-growing movement. And not one I care to join.

For I do have the strange, audacious belief that the implanted word of the incarnate One can save my life. Your life. Their lives.

Sermon Two

Rev. Brian K. Blount, PhD currently serves as the president and professor of New Testament at Union Presbyterian Seminary in Richmond, Virginia. Brian's work crossing the areas of New Testament and Preaching is well-known, especially his Beecher Lectures at Yale Divinity School that resulted in the book *Invasion of the Dead: Preaching Resurrection*.[3] Those familiar with that work will see some similar themes here, in addition to Brian's work with the book of Revelation.

His sermon, entitled "Live Your Life Like It Means Something," is based on Revelation 12:10-11 and was preached for a weekly chapel service at Union Presbyterian Seminary in November 2017. It displays well the concept of radical imagination and uses the movie *It's a Wonderful Life* and contemporary examples as places that operate as disimagination machines. While Brian's sermon conveys information about the book of Revelation, which many find difficult (even seminary students!) and about the literary-theological nature of apocalyptic literature, this sermon is not for the purposes of conveying information to listeners but rather for the purposes of emancipatory transformation.

"Live Your Life Like It Means Something"—Revelation 12:10-11

Months ago, I was in my closet, fiddling with the button on the right sleeve of my dress shirt, that one that is so doggone difficult, when another piece of the book of Revelation came clear for me. Unlike what happened with John, there was nothing special about the time or place of this unveiling. When John received his revelation, a door opened and he found himself in heaven. I found myself in the closet. Not the Lord's Day. Just a run-of-the-mill Thursday. John got lightning and thunder. I got the dim glow of a sixty-watt bulb. For some reason, standing there in my closet, wishing I were still in bed, I glimpsed a vision...from the movie *It's a Wonderful Life*.

I've never really liked *It's a Wonderful Life*. First, it's in black and white. I'm sorry, but God created the world in technicolor for a reason. Second, the thing makes no sense. As an exposé on the movie reported this past Christmas season, when old Mr. Potter practically steals money from George Bailey and puts George about $8,000 in debt, something more is going on than an old meanie stealing money. At the end of the movie, when it looks like George is bankrupt because of that lost $8,000, the good news is that George's friend wires in a line of credit for $25,000. That's only good news when you don't think about what has just happened. What has just happened is that George, once $8,000 in debt, is now $33,000 in debt. Two days after Christmas, he'll stop singing Christmas carols and start singing the blues. Third thing is, I don't like Clarence the angel. What kind of angel name is Clarence? I don't have anything against the name Clarence. It's a great name. Like Brian. I love the name Brian. It's *my* name. But whoever thinks of an angel named Brian? Michael. Gabriel. Raphael. Those are angel names. But Clarence? To make matters even worse, Clarence is an old, tottering, teetering, almost fool of a guy. That's not how an angel looks. An angel is supposed to be the Terminator with wings. I can't watch a movie where the angel looks like he's the weakest person in the promotion. But that morning in the closet, I got it.

It's a Wonderful Life is an apocalyptic story. It's hiding something beneath all the silliness of Pottersville. Apocalyptic materials reveal something dramatically outrageous about the future, forcing us to live with a dramatically outrageous sense of urgency in the present.

> Through the lens of the movie, Brian begins to set up qualities of what I have called the preacher-as-teacher's "radical imagination." This is a function of the kind of apocalyptic literature found in the book of Revelation.

Clarence the angel shows George Bailey something outrageously dramatic about the future. You know the story. The angel reveals what the future would look like if George had never been born, so that George will see the meaning and urgency of his present. Unbeknownst to George, he, not Mr. Potter, was the most powerful man in the town. Without George, the town would have been devastated. George turned out to be the one thing standing between a town living and a town dying. *That's* why you can't jump off the bridge and commit suicide, George. *That* is *why* God placed you where God placed you, in the time that God placed you, amidst the struggles God did not protect you from, George. God needed you to be the kind of man you were in the past, so you could create hope for the people of Pottersville present and future. *It's*

> Brian introduces here the relationship of believers to the public sphere. The conversational rhetorical style leads us to an important place of ecclesiology. Notice the "we" and "us" language.

a Wonderful Life was also attempting to convince us that the truth about George Bailey is the truth about each one of us. Without us playing the part God would have us play, some part of our world would be devastated.

Which brings me back to the book of Revelation. It reveals something dramatically outrageous about the future that intends to make us live with more dramatic urgency in the present.

In God's future, Jesus sees a world where…

…lepers are touched.

…women are equals and are not physically and psychologically abused.

…the powerless are empowered.

…resources are shared.

…the hungry are not only fed, but the systems that create and perpetuate hunger are destroyed.

> Brian names features of a public sphere characterized by the *basileia tou Theou* in the book of Revelation and beyond. This is radical imagination ("dramatically outrageous")! What follows is an excellent rhetorical "run." Alternatively, I wonder if Brian might have employed a story from Revelation or the Gospels rather than painting with a broad brush.

…the demonic powers are defeated.

…those who have been thrown low by life are lifted up by friends and strangers alike.

…the doors to the house of prayer are open to every person from every station and condition in life.

…access to the potency of God's love is boundless and open to everyone who would seek it.

Having seen this dramatically outrageous future, God's future, Jesus sets about dramatically and urgently transforming his present so that people can live that future right now.

That is the apocalyptic mandate: having seen the future, *create* the future in the here and now. And it will take much patience, perseverance, faith, struggle, and failure, because

> As we saw earlier in Brian's own writing, this is a feature of Jesus as teacher, where his teaching was embodied action and not a just transfer of biblical or theological content. The teacher is one who performs the word. Additionally, Brian begins to addresses resistance.

the powers that rule the present do not want to give way to the change demanded by God's future. In the book of Revelation, John shows us cataclysm for a reason. The cataclysms are the by-product of God's engagement with the powers who rule our present, who threaten to take over and decimate our world, by preventing its transformation into God's world. The *de*struction John sees is actually the result of God's ultimately *con*structive fight. God is fighting for God's future in the midst of our present.

That is why, according to John the Revelator, God calls *us* to stand up and witness with God for God's future in the midst of the present, to witness for the kind of world God intends in the face of institutions, peoples, and powers who prefer to maintain and manipulate the world we have. Like the angel Clarence, John wants to maintain that every little thing we do has an impact in breaking down the devastation that the powers of evil want to wreak in the world (12:10-11).

Hear what might be the most critical verse in the entire book of the Revelation to John: *They* (John's people) conquered *him* (the greatest power against God that ever existed), by the blood of the Lamb *and* by the word of their witness to the lordship of that same bloodied Lamb. By their witness. The "they" are the people of faith who populate his churches. The "him" is the dragon. We are talking incarnational evil, the source of all the horror of our world. This is the same "him" whom only God, one would guess, has enough power to take on. It takes not just an angel, but an archangel to throw him out of heaven. This is no job for an angel like Clarence. We're talking Michael. No ordinary angel. Once this force is thrown out of heaven, one would think no ordinary human can take him on. And yet, John says, *they* do! His *ordinary* humans take on the infestation of evil and conquer it. Do you hear what John is saying? That *they* is *us*. *We* have that kind of power in *us*. That is the truth that the book of Revelation reveals.

> Brian begins here to name the agency believers have to engage in emancipatory practice. He will begin below to raise up courage, based on confidence in God's death-defeating power, as a value by which believers can work for change.

You know how some athletes talk trash? There are some who can back up what they say, so they say it when they feel they need to say it. That's the right time to talk trash: when your opponent isn't quite sure, you help the doubt grow by telling him he's not as good as he thinks he is. It was game one of the NBA Finals, 1997. The Chicago Bulls versus the Utah Jazz. It was in the final seconds of the game. The score was 84-82. Karl Malone was the Most Valuable Player of the league that year. They called him the Mailman because he always came through. He'd just been fouled and was on the line, ready to take his free throws and tie the game. Scottie Pippin of the Bulls was walking past Malone, and as he walked passed, he whispered, "Just remember, the Mailman doesn't deliver on Sundays." Trash. Talk.

Why the talk? To let him know that you can see the future and the future ends with him down and you up. You got the nerve to live like that in this world where it looks like God's people and God's causes are often down and destructive causes and destructive people are often up? You got the nerve to look at them and the situations they perpetuate and say, "I can see the future. God owns the future. And God has already given the future to me. God's future will win. Your design for the future will lose. I know it"?

> Giving listeners permission to use these bold, confident words for themselves could be characterized as an act of plain speech.

That is essentially the testimony John is telling his trash talkers to testify: God beat every power, every person who would oppose God's design for this world when God raised Jesus. And God's going to beat you again when God raises *me* up whenever you or the forces that work for you try to put one of God's people or God's causes down. You *can* walk that talk because you don't walk alone. God, John says, walks with you. Go out into the world and talk some God trash talk.

Step up...

...to the politicians who refuse to build budgets that provide for people in need and tell them that you're coming for them.

...to the children thinking about dropping out of school that they ain't dropping nothing until you give them permission.

> Here the preacher-as-teacher uses plain speech to communicate real actions believers might take to work against the disimagination machines of government and cultured despair among youth.

...and open up your mouth, then put your faith and your resources where your trash talking is.

Like George Bailey, if we see what the world would be like without our witness, we will see tragedy and devastation. George Bailey was fictional. Our real lives are at least as important as George Bailey's fictitious life. Our present witness is every bit as important as John of Patmos's past witness. Without our witness, our world will be devastated. Just like Clarence scared George straight off that bridge where he wanted to give away his life *back* into a community where he could devote his life to helping others, John wants to scare us right out of our sanctuaries and into the world.

Brian imagines believers as fully engaged in the public sphere with whatever agency they can muster. There is urgency as well to engage the ongoing and possible devastation. The book of Revelation, so often explained (taught) in sermons for understanding a difficult book, functions with rhetorical urgency for the community's life and witness. The word "devastation" has come up a few times now and I wonder if Brian might parse that out even more for us. What does devastation look like for us if it is different from the book of Revelation's depiction.

In *The Diary of a Young Girl*, Anne Frank, is revealed as a heroine whose sheer existence witnessed against the satanic powers behind the Nazi Holocaust. She wrote: "How wonderful it is that no one has to wait a single moment to change the world." John challenges his people to rise *up* and rise *into* every single moment. This moment where the greatest force that has ever stared down humankind, now roaming and terrorizing the earth, caught up in its own glory, living itself out in poverty, homelessness, spiritual brokenness, political gridlock, economic and military

Again, Brian names for us the components of the disimagination machine, forwarding his critique.

imperialism, the devastation of people desperately seeking hope in a world that seems hopeless all across our globe and right here.

This moment…*every moment*…is *our* George Bailey moment. If we stand up and face the forces that furiously feed on God's people and do what *we* can, large or small, to make a difference. *We* can conquer *him* by the blood of the Lamb and the force of our witness.

That is why it matters…

…what you do the moment you walk out of this building.

…that you respond the next time someone reaches out to you for help.

…that with all the world's great big problems, you can make a great big difference even if the difference you make seems small by comparison.

…that you come to church to get a glimpse of God's dramatically outrageous future and then walk urgently out of this church with the defiant determination to drag a piece of that heavenly future into this hellacious present.

Our story *is* an apocalyptic story. Just as the angel Clarence wanted to show something miraculous to the mild-mannered George Bailey, so John the Revelator wants to reveal something outrageous to you: you are the most important person in God's story. So live your life like it means something. No, live your life like it means everything.

This is another wonderful rhetorical run by which Brian carries forward the apocalyptic urgency he has communicated throughout the sermon. And he again employs the language of "dramatically outrageous future."

But I wonder, since we have built up a large amount of critique, if he could be even more concrete here by showing us how communities of faith are building resistance, possibility/hope, and living into the radical imagination.

This is a small note, but one that I believe makes a difference. Brian begins with the first-person plural "our story." But then he changes it to the second-personal singular "you" and "yours." In imagining our story as a collective one, I imagine an even more effective call to us would be to maintain the first-person plural, keeping it consistent with John's address to the churches.

85

Sermon 3

The final sermon is one of my own, which I preached as a guest at Ginter Park Presbyterian Church, a PC(USA) congregation in Richmond, Virginia. I preached this sermon in the weeks after the shooting at Marjory Stoneman Douglas High School in Parkland, Florida, and during the season of Lent. The scripture passage comes from John 18:12-27, which is featured in the Narrative Lectionary. In terms of a teaching sermon, it sought to help listeners form a social imagination patterned after Jesus's own actions as the passion narrative begins to unfold. In order to speak about some taboos like gun violence and the Black Lives Matter movement, I develop the idea of the faithfulness of Jesus in the midst of chaos as a pattern seen elsewhere in our contemporary world. I also name the alternative imagination of the reign of God found in Jesus's life as a worthy way of patterning our lives.

"Faithful Resolve"—John 18:12-27

I doubt you worry much about this, but if we were following what has become a more traditional group of readings called the Revised Common Lectionary, typically at this point in Lent we'd probably be watching Jesus getting into that "good trouble" of driving the money changers out of the temple. But you all are using the Narrative Lectionary, which is constructed a bit differently. And when Carla asked me to preach this passage from John, I agreed without hesitation and without looking at the text. And then I read it. And I remembered that this is typically a Good Friday text. And after I read it, over and over and over again my brain and my soul said, "Hold on, just a minute! Too soon." Now don't point fingers, but some of you still have your Christmas lights up. We are not that many weeks removed from the Christmas season and Epiphany, the very beginnings of Jesus's life and ministry.

> Commentary on the differing lectionaries makes for an atypical introduction, but I believe the congregation was attentive to this dynamic since they had an explanation about the Narrative Lectionary in their bulletin. The intention was to introduce the Scripture passage—as it occurred in the cycle of time—as an unexpected, disruptive intervention for me.

But now here we are, the third week of Lent, and as disorienting as it might be, Jesus has been arrested and handed over to Annas. He is questioned and assaulted. Meanwhile, as Peter warms himself by the fire, when he is questioned as to whether he is one of Jesus's followers, he responds with those cold words, "I am not."

But perhaps it's not so much the timing that makes it too soon. It's not as if we don't know that this happens to Jesus. We've heard this story plenty of times before. So maybe it's that this passage comes amidst our own cultural chaos. There's enough upheaval and topsy-turvy going in our world that we can do without this story encroaching upon our safe church spaces. At least not yet. Not until we get to Holy Week where we might normally see this story race by us. At this point in our Lenten journey we have to deal with this text and the chaos that's here for Jesus. Not later. Now. We are thrust into the chaos of Jesus's final days.

It's not unlike William Butler Yeats's famous poem "The Second Coming." You may know it, especially that first stanza:

Turning and turning in the
    widening gyre
The falcon cannot hear the
    falconer;
Things fall apart; the center
    cannot hold;
Mere anarchy is loosed
    upon the world,
The blood-dimmed tide is
    loosed, and everywhere
The ceremony of innocence
    is drowned;
The best lack all convic-
    tion, while the worst
Are full of passionate intensity.

> The feeling I get from reading the passage in the third week of Lent led me down the road of exploring the reasons why this passage felt so odd outside of the time in which it was read. The analogue of chaos in the biblical text and the Yeats poem provide an avenue toward understanding how I experienced the passage and opens the way toward critique.

Yeats began the poem in January 1919, on the heels of World War I, the revolution in Russia, and political upheaval in Yeats's own Ireland. Throughout the poem Yeats produces a thick representation of the anxiety, unrest, and violence he saw in the world. And Yeats was unnerved by what one writer called the loss of "societal structures; the loss of collective religious faith, and with it, the collective sense of purpose; the feeling that the old rules no longer apply and there's nothing to replace them."[4]

Perhaps we can feel the anxiety of Yeats's poem in John's Gospel narrative. Here stands Jesus, whose ministry of healing and restoring and feeding and teaching comes to a full and abrupt stop. He is bound...restrained. John drops us into the middle of chaotic rupture, anxiety, loss, violence.

> Things fall apart; the center cannot hold.
> Mere anarchy is loosed upon the world,
> the blood-dimmed tide is loosed, and everywhere
> the ceremony of innocence is drowned.

And then we see Peter and Annas with the authorities: "the best lack all conviction, while the worst are full of passionate intensity."

Annas and Peter are woven together with Jesus in this fascinating narrative.

> Here I begin critique of the biblical characters in earnest. They will function as possible types for our modern-day lives of faith. I set up the critique through a type of narrative equivalence. Annas comes first.

You cannot have any of these characters without the other here in this passage. On the one hand, you have Annas, the high priest. John's readers know that Annas and his father-in-law Caiaphas have already passed their judgment on Jesus back in chapter 11. He will die. This appearance is a formality at best. It's a sham designed to cover themselves, to justify their pre-determination: "We questioned him! And still he wouldn't fall in line!" The dangerous cooperation between religious and political power work death on this innocent, vulnerable man. The idea is to pacify Jesus and to consolidate whatever power is available to himself. Annas and his associates are jockeying for respectability and power. And above all, Annas must prove that he is not disposable. The problem with Jesus is clear: If you want to know who represents God, who can speak to God's interests, and where it concerns Rome, who can keep the faithful in line, Annas says, "I can. Watch me." Annas chooses a religious and political form of collusion that secures his place in the power structure. Jesus is simply the collateral damage.

On the other hand, here's Peter.

We know all about Peter. He and the other disciple follow Jesus in verse 15: follow—that's discipleship language. But this is as faithful as it gets. Peter's discipleship in this moment is limited to geographical proximity. He pulls up a comfy pew by the fire outside the gate. But that is as far as he will go. Not making Annas's choice, but not making the choice of a faithful disciple either. In this moment, Peter chooses the relative safety of denial. Disassociation is the best form of self-preservation, you know.

> Peter comes second.

It is not without accident that these two are woven together. These seem to be the dangerous poles ever before us. These two possibilities are the enduring haunt of this scripture. It's not that we are people who give it the good old college try in our faith and come up short. No, the possibility is that like Peter we might be deniers, that we might be deserters of the cause, that we might be full of

> Here I want to suggest that there are two ways that the radical imagination can become coopted by the disimagination machine: through moments of zeal followed by apathy and also by collusion with or accommodation to the powerful in order to reinforce our own lives. This comes as plain speech as well, as most of us can probably identify with one of these poles or the other. However, I am not as concrete here as I could have been in describing how these manifest in our lives.

fiery zeal, hoisting protest signs in one chapter of our faith but warming our cold hearts by the fire saying, "Not me" in the next. The other possibility is that like Annas we become co-conspirators in the kind of religious expression that does violence to others and smugly identifies it as God's will. Perhaps in our knowledge of the public record of Jesus, we become adept at twisting it and contorting it to reinforce our position...to benefit ourselves...to make our version of

> I have introduced critique in Peter and Annas. Now I introduce possibility/hope in a similar literary manner through Jesus' actions.

faith triumphant. If we're not careful, if we're not vigilant, then we might just become Peter or Annas.

Notice that I say that these stories are woven. In the middle of Peter and Annas, there stands Jesus.

Forget for a moment your notions that Jesus had some kind of super-power that made him immune to the trauma of these moments. Disabuse yourselves of that idea that Jesus had the capacity to rise about the terror of what is starting to unfold. Arrested, bound, and carted from one place to the next as a prisoner. Publicly humiliated and assaulted. His coalition of would-be followers is faltering.

And yet. Jesus. Will. Not. Be. Moved. Jesus will not be deterred. If there was a time for Jesus to step back, to reassess, and moderate things a bit, now's the time. But no. He continues to hold fast when things fall apart. "Everything I've said has been in public. In full view. If you haven't heard, go ask somebody," Jesus responds firmly.

Jesus chooses faithful resolve to live into the reign of God over accommodation to the powers that be.

While the centers of power choose passionate intensity and Peter loses all conviction, Jesus chooses faithful, unwavering resolve to the realm of God. This is not redemptive suffering. This is holding fast to the ways of the realm of God no matter what may come. This is faithful witness. Jesus stands in solidarity with all those who suffer at the hands of the powerful. In his faithfulness in this moment,

> I intentionally invoke language of the *basileia tou Theou* since allegiances are especially present in the text. One possible problem with this, however, is that the language of the *basileia tou Theou* occurs infrequently in the Gospel of John, and not in this passage. The language I inherit from the Synoptics transfers here.

> Here I name "alternative imagination" as a way of denoting the "radical imagination." But I do not spell out well enough what Jesus's faithfulness exists as an alternative *to*, even as I mention "the pretensions of power and position." I could have been more concrete in laying this out. Shorthand for the radical imagination, especially in a guest preaching situation, does little good.

Jesus exercises an alternative imagination, declaring that the ways of God's steadfast love for all can bring healing and wholeness, far beyond the pretensions of power and position.

And when we see Jesus's faithfulness in this moment, when we hear him speak, I cannot help but see and hear the young students from Parkland, Florida, who have burst onto the national scene these past few weeks: Emma Gonzalez, Cameron Kasky, David Hogg, Jaclyn Corin, Alex Wind, Delaney Tarr, and so many others.

We all would have understood if they took their trauma into the shadows. We would have understood if they would have shrunk back when the internet trolls came to attack and when the would-be adults came to call them crisis actors and doubt their capacity or maturity

I want to frame border pedagogy and fugitive forms of knowledge here. Their courage after tragedy displayed the kind of radical imagination that addresses resistance.

to speak truth to power. If after the first day of outrage, they'd mourned their friends and returned to a quiet life, we would all have simply shrugged our shoulders and said, "Well, it was a nice try. Those kids showed some pluck. Good for them." But here we are, two and a half weeks later in a twenty-four-hour news cycle world. And still they will not be deterred from creating a world where access to the weapons of war are off our streets. Still they look into the cameras with resolve and tell us #NeverAgain. Still they are not deterred from calling us away from mistaking guns for God.

Their resolve and their courage is not theirs alone, though.

It is the resolve of those young people who took to the streets of Sanford, Florida, and Ferguson, Missouri, who raised their voices to say that their lives—black lives—*really matter*. To declare with unmovable resolve that the conditions for their lives are ones in which they

Here I want to enable listeners as critical thinkers about a kind of genealogy of faithful courage and naming what I thought may have been taboo topics. By rooting the Parkland students' courage in the Black Lives Matter movement and beyond that, to the civil rights movement, I suggest a common well for courageous, emancipatory praxis rooted in the alternative imagination of the basileia tou Theou.

are deemed worthless, unless it is for their cheap labor, disposable unless they can benefit those who sit at the top of the ladder. And to demand more.

It is the same resolve of those young people who sat down on busses and at lunch counters while the fire hoses screamed and walked into schools while white people spat and dogs' teeth flashed, ready to devour. It is the resolve of all those who locked arms and walked across bridges and into the halls of state capitols, and of all those who have sung both then and now, "ain't gonna let nobody turn me around…gonna keep on walking, keep on talking, marching to freedom land."

> The connections and identification strengthen here. I also name the radical imagination as an ideal.

Maybe you hear Jesus. "If I have spoken wrongly, testify to the wrong. But if I have spoken rightly, why do you strike me? Nevertheless, I'm gonna keep on walking, keep on talking, marching up to freedom land." Maybe in them you hear Jesus. The faithful resolve of Jesus continues to speak among us now with the radical, determined imagination of the kingdom of God.

Maybe this text is not too soon for us. No, maybe it's right on time. Because this is what Lent asks of us: "What will you choose? When things fall apart, which way will you go? What will you choose?" The first words of the ancient Christian document the *Didache* say that there are two ways, one of life and one of death, but a great difference between the two ways. Nowhere is that clearer than when Jesus stands before Annas, with Peter outside the gate.

> Here I name possibility/hope as a value for us to live into over the enticement of the disimagination machine with the design "to make despair unconvincing and hope practical." However, the ending here is not as concrete as it could be. To a great extent, this fault is a function of being a guest preacher and not being in mutual conversation with the people of this congregation. In these situations, I hope to avoid any signs of authoritarianism in my claims. On the other hand, I do live in the same city, so I cannot blame my lack of specificity and call for the congregation on my outsider status.

In the face of anarchy and the blood-dimmed tide swelling

around him, Jesus chooses to stand by the words and deeds of the realm of God:

> Peace over violence.
> Love over hate.
> Solidarity over separation.
> In a chaotic and crisis-filled moment,
> Jesus chooses to stand with those who suffer,
>   with those who are being crushed,
>   with those who are vulnerable.
> He chooses to stand, undeterred.
> Oh, church, let that be us!

Lent calls us to no less of a decision: to choose which way we will go, to decide which path we will take.

When things fall apart, when the center does not hold, may it be said of us that we stood faithfully like Jesus, who would not be moved. Amen.

Notes

Introduction

1. "GA-1521-Substitute Resolution on Gun Violence.Pdf," accessed August 9, 2017, http://disciples.org/wp-content/uploads/2011/01/GA-1521-Substitute-Resolution-on-Gun -Violence.pdf.

2. George Lakoff and Mark Johnson, *Metaphors We Live By* (Chicago: Univ. of Chicago Press, 2011).

3. Thomas G Long, *The Witness of Preaching*, 2nd ed. (Louisville, KY: Westminster John Knox Press, 2005).

4. Jana Childers, ed., *Birthing the Sermon: Women Preachers on the Creative Process* (St. Louis, MO: Chalice Press, 2001), ix.

5. Alyce McKenzie, *Hear and Be Wise: Becoming a Preacher and Teacher of Wisdom* (Nashville: Abingdon Press, 2004).

6. Robert Stephen Reid, ed., *Slow of Speech and Unclean Lips: Contemporary Images of Preaching Identity* (Eugene, OR: Wipf & Stock Pub, 2010).

7. Kenyatta R. Gilbert, *The Journey and Promise of African American Preaching* (Minneapolis, MN: Fortress Press, 2011).

8. Ronald J. Allen and O. Wesley Allen Jr., *The Sermon without End: A Conversational Approach to Preaching* (Nashville: Abingdon Press, 2015); O. Wesley Allen, John McClure, and Ronald J. Allen, eds., *Under the Oak Tree: The Church as Community of Conversation in a Conflicted and Pluralistic World* (Eugene, OR: Cascade Books, 2013).

9. Augustine, "On Christian Doctrine, in Four Books: Christian Classics Ethereal Library," accessed August 9, 2017, https://www.ccel.org/ccel/augustine/doctrine.i.html.

10. Book 4, Chapter 11, Augustine.

11. Alan of Lille, as quoted in O. C. Edwards, *A History of Preaching*, 1st ed. (Nashville: Abingdon Press, 2004), 178.

12. Jean Calvin, *Calvin: Institutes of the Christian Religion, Book IV*, (Louisville, KY: Westminster John Knox Press, 2006), Chapter 1.5.

13. Calvin, *Book IV*, Chapter 3.4 .

14. Granville T. Walker, *Preaching in the Thought of Alexander Campbell* (Bloomington, MN: Bethany Press, 1954), 158.

15. Alexander Campbell, as quoted in Walker, *Preaching in the Thought of Alexander Campbell* 158.

16. C. H. (Charles Harold) Dodd, *The Apostolic Preaching and Its Developments: Three Lectures with an Appendix on Eschatology and History* (New York: Harper, 1936).

17. Robert C. Worley, *Preaching and Teaching in the Earliest Church* (Westminster Press, 1967), 21.

18. For a more thorough discussion of why this distinction does not hold, see Worley, 30–86.

19. Calvin, *Book IV*, Chapter 3.4.

20. Clark M. Williamson and Ronald J. Allen, *The Teaching Minister* (Louisville, KY: Westminster John Knox Press, 1991), 7.

21. Ronald J. Allen, *The Teaching Sermon* (Nashville: Abingdon Press, 1995), 16, 18.

22. Thomas G. Long, *Preaching from Memory to Hope* (Louisville, KY: Westminster John Knox Press, 2009), 5–6.

23. Alyce M. McKenzie, *Novel Preaching: Tips from Top Writers on Crafting Creative Sermons* (Westminster John Knox Press, 2010), 2.

24. We do not have the space here to unpack fully the reasoning for this switch in terminology, which occurs mostly in nondenominational and evangelical circles. I believe it has largely to do with the sense that people are increasingly in need of instruction (biblical and theological illiteracy) and that there is an aversion to naming that event as preaching out of fear of the connotations it might have for those who are unchurched or *dechurched*.

25. McKenzie, *Novel Preaching*, 6.

26. Robert Stephen Reid, *The Four Voices of Preaching* (Ada, MI: Brazos Press, 2006), 53.

27. Paul Scott Wilson, *Setting Words on Fire: Putting God at the Center of the Sermon* (Nashville: Abingdon Press, 2008), 17.

28. Wilson, 25.

29. Wilson, 82.

30. See, for instance, Thomas G. Long, "And How Shall They Hear? The Listener in Contemporary Preaching," Gail R. O'Day and Thomas G. Long, eds., *Listening to the Word: Studies in Honor of Fred B. Craddock* (Nashville: Abingdon Press, 1993), 167–88.

31. Allen, *The Teaching Sermon*, 28.

32. Paulo Freire, *Pedagogy of the Oppressed* (New York: Continuum, 2000).

33. Peter McLaren and Joe L. Kincheloe, eds., *Critical Pedagogy: Where Are We Now?* (New York: Peter Lang Inc., International Academic Publishers, 2007), 17.

34. Henry A. Giroux, "Educated Hope in Dark Times: The Challenge of the Educator-Artist as a Public Intellectual," Truthout, accessed April 11, 2018, http://www.truth-out.org/news/item/44081-educated-hope-in-dark-times-the-challenge-of-the-educator-artist-as-a-public-intellectual.

Chapter 1

1. bell hooks, *Teaching to Transgress: Education as the Practice of Freedom* (New York: Routledge, 1994), 12.

2. Thomas G. Long, "When the Preacher Is a Teacher," *Journal for Preachers* 16, no. 2 (1993): 21.

3. Long, 22.

4. Long, 22.

5. Paulo Freire, *Pedagogy of the Oppressed* (New York: Continuum, 2000), 72.

6. Freire, 73.

7. Freire, 73.

8. Paulo Freire and Henry A. Giroux, *The Politics of Education: Culture, Power and Liberation*, trans. Donaldo Macedo, 1st edition (South Hadley, MA: Bergin & Garvey Publishers, 1985), 46.

9. Freire, *Pedagogy of the Oppressed*, 81.

10. Henry A. Giroux, *Teachers as Intellectuals: Toward a Critical Pedagogy of Learning* (Granby, MA: Praeger, 1988), 125.

11. Giroux, 123.

12. Giroux, 125.

13. hooks, *Teaching to Transgress*, 59–75. I will say more about this in chapter 4.

14. Giroux, *Teachers as Intellectuals*, 10.

15. Joe L. Kincheloe, *Critical Pedagogy Primer*, 4th edition (New York: Peter Lang Inc., International Academic Publishers, 2008), 73.

16. Giroux, *Teachers as Intellectuals*, 126.

17. Giroux, 127.

18. Peter McLaren, "Foreward: Critical Theory and the Meaning of Hope" in Giroux, xvii.

19. Henry A. Giroux, *On Critical Pedagogy* (New York: Bloomsbury, 2011), 72.

20. Gallup Inc, "Sermon Content Is What Appeals Most to Churchgoers," Gallup.com, n.d., http://www.gallup.com/poll/208529/sermon-content-appeals-churchgoers.aspx.

21. Leonora Tubbs Tisdale, *Prophetic Preaching: A Pastoral Approach* (Louisville, KY: Westminster John Knox, 2010), 11–20.

22. Tisdale, 20.

23. Harry Emerson Fosdick, "What Is the Matter with Preaching?" *Harper's* (July 1928): 133–141, reprinted in Mike Graves, *What's the Matter with Preaching Today?* (Louisville, KY: Westminster John Knox, 2004), 10.

24. Giroux, *Teachers as Intellectuals*, 126.

25. Katie Geneva Cannon, *Katie's Cannon.* (New York: Continuum: 2003), 116. See also "Traditional and Critical Theory" in Max Horkheimer and Stanley Aronowitz, Critical Theory: Selected Essays, trans. Matthew J. O'Connell, first edition (New York: Continuum, 1975), 188–243.

26. Henry A. Giroux, "Democracy, Education, and the Politics of Critical Pedagogy," in Peter McLaren and Joe L. Kincheloe, eds., *Critical Pedagogy: Where Are We Now?* (New York: Peter Lang International Academic, 2007), 3.

27. Giroux, *Teachers as Intellectuals*, 127.

28. Thomas H. Groome, *Christian Religious Education: Sharing Our Story and Vision* (San Francisco: Jossey-Bass, 1999).

29. Katie Geneva Cannon, *Katie's Canon: Womanism and the Soul of Black Community* (Continuum: New York, 2003), 116. Emphasis mine.

30. hooks, *Teaching to Transgress*, 19.

31. Elsewhere I use the term *homiletic communities* as a way of describing communities that think about preaching together. See Richard W. Voelz, *Youthful Preaching: Strengthening the Relationship between Youth, Adults, and Preaching* (Eugene, OR: Cascade Books, 2016).

32. I will say more about what I mean by "emancipatory practices and transformation" in subsequent chapters.

33. Giroux, *Teachers as Intellectuals*, 151.

34. Giroux, 150–51.

35. hooks, *Teaching to Transgress*, 19.

36. Giroux notes in places the impact of liberation theology and feminist theology on Freire's work and, therefore, the larger project of critical pedagogy. And Peter McLaren's work places liberation theology in a much more prominent place than Giroux.

37. Giroux, *Teachers as Intellectuals*, 123–25.

38. Giroux, 123.

39. Giroux, 123–24.

40. Giroux uses the term "teacher-proof" to describe curriculum packages that "reserves

for teachers the role of simply carrying out predetermined content and instructional procedures." Giroux, 124.

41. Bonnie J. Miller-McLemore, *Christian Theology in Practice: Discovering a Discipline* (Grand Rapids, MI: Eerdmans, 2012), 164–66. Miller-McLemore's detailed chapters in this book outline important arguments to which I will only point. It will have to suffice to point to them here, with the point being that there is significant discussion over what constitutes practical theological education and how one learns ministerial practices like preaching.

42. Giroux, *Teachers as Intellectuals*, 124.

Chapter 2

1. From Giroux's March 29, 2018, keynote address at the University of Waterloo in Ontario, Canada.

2. "Preaching in the Purple Zone," accessed April 13, 2018, https://thepurplezone.net/preaching-in-purple-zone.

3. Christian Smith and Melina Lundquist Denton, *Soul Searching: The Religious and Spiritual Lives of American Teenagers*, reprint edition (Oxford: Oxford University Press, 2009).

4. David J. Lose, *Preaching at the Crossroads: How the World—and Our Preaching—Is Changing* (Minneapolis, MN: Fortress, 2013), 51.

5. Peter McLaren, "Foreward: Critical Theory and the Meaning of Hope" in Henry A. Giroux, *Teachers as Intellectuals: Toward a Critical Pedagogy of Learning* (Granby, MA: Praeger, 1988), xvii. Italics are mine.

6. Henry A. Giroux, *Theory and Resistance in Education: Towards a Pedagogy for the Opposition*, 2nd ed. (Westport, CT: Praeger, 2001), 242.

7. Giroux, 242.

8. Giroux, 242.

9. Giroux, 239.

10. Jennifer M. McBride, *Radical Discipleship: A Liturgical Politics of the Gospel* (Minneapolis, MN: Fortress Press, 2017).

11. J. Randall Nichols, *The Restoring Word: Preaching as Pastoral Communication* (Eugene, OR: Wipf & Stock Pub, 2003), 103.

12. Richard W. Voelz, *Youthful Preaching: Strengthening the Relationship between Youth, Adults, and Preaching* (Eugene, OR: Cascade Books, 2016).

13. John S. McClure, "The Other Side of Sermon Illustration," *Journal for Preachers* 12, no. 2 (1989): 2–4.

14. O. Wesley Allen Jr., *The Homiletic of All Believers: A Conversational Approach to Proclamation and Preaching*, 1st ed. (Louisville, KY: Westminster John Knox, 2005), 49.

15. Allen Jr., 47–48.

16. H. Richard Niebuhr, *Christ and Culture*, reprint edition (San Francisco: Harper & Row, 1975).

17. Burton Z. Cooper and John S. McClure, *Claiming Theology in the Pulpit* (Louisville, KY: Westminster John Knox Press, 2003), 47–55; McClure presents a similar, though slightly different scheme in an earlier published work: John S. McClure, *The Four Codes of Preaching: Rhetorical Strategies* (Louisville, KY: Westminster John Knox, 2004).

18. Leonora Tubbs Tisdale, *Preaching as Local Theology and Folk Art* (Minneapolis, MN: Fortress, 1997), 83.

19. Tisdale, 84.

20. Tisdale, 84.

21. Charles L. Campbell, *The Word Before the Powers: An Ethic of Preaching*, 1st ed., (Louisville, KY: Westminster John Knox, 2002).

22. Campbell, 2–3.

23. Though to be fair, in his more recent work Campbell engages the image of the fool for preaching and its role in public spaces. See Charles L. Campbell and Johan H. Cilliers, *Preaching Fools: The Gospel as a Rhetoric of Folly* (Waco, TX: Baylor University Press, 2012), 68ff.

24. Campbell, *The Word Before the Powers*, 123.

25. Campbell, 125. I will have more to say about imagination in the next chapter.

26. Campbell, 184.

27. See for instance David Buttrick, *Preaching the New and the Now* (Louisville, KY: Westminster John Knox, 1998); Kathryn Tanner, *Theories of Culture: A New Agenda for Theology* (Minneapolis, MN: Fortress, 1997).

28. Kenyatta R. Gilbert, *A Pursued Justice: Black Preaching from the Great Migration to Civil Rights* (Waco, TX: Baylor University Press, 2016), 65.

29. Gilbert, 69.

30. Gilbert, 70.

31. William J. Barber II and Barbara Zelter, *Forward Together: A Moral Message for the Nation* (St. Louis, MO: Chalice, 2014), 12.

32. Barber II and Zelter, 12.

33. "Poor People's Campaign: A National Call for Moral Revival," Poor People's Campaign, accessed June 11, 2018, https://www.poorpeoplescampaign.org/.

34. Barber II and Zelter, *Forward Together*, 19.35.

35. Buttrick, *Preaching the New and the Now*, 107.

36. Greg Carey, "The King of the Jews and the Kin-Dom of God (Matthew 2:1-12)," *The Christian Century*, accessed February 1, 2018, https://www.christiancentury.org/blog-post/sundays-coming/king-jews-and-kin-dom-god-matthew-21-12.

37. Brian K. Blount, *Go Preach!: Mark's Kingdom Message and the Black Church Today* (Maryknoll, NY: Orbis, 1998).

38. Buttrick, *Preaching the New and the Now*, 7.

39. Blount, *Go Preach!*, 17.

40. Buttrick, *Preaching the New and the Now*, 13.

41. Buttrick, 17.

42. Blount, *Go Preach!*, 23.

43. Buttrick, *Preaching the New and the Now*, 13.

44. Blount, *Go Preach!*, 84.

45. Blount, 180.

46. Here I echo both David Buttrick and Thomas Long who in different keys suggest that biblical texts have intentions or functions (in their rhetorical form or performative force). See for instance David Buttrick, *Homiletic: Moves and Structures* (Philadelphia, PA: Fortress, 1987); Thomas G. Long, *Preaching and the Literary Forms of the Bible* (Philadelphia: Fortress, 1988).

Chapter 3

1. Paulo Freire, *Pedagogy of Hope: Reliving Pedagogy of the Oppressed* (New York: Bloomsbury, 2014), 3.

2. Henry A. Giroux, *On Critical Pedagogy* (New York: Bloomsbury, 2011), 5.

3. Giroux, 5.

4. bell hooks, *Teaching to Transgress: Education as the Practice of Freedom* (New York: Routledge, 1994), 29.

5. hooks, 30. For hooks, when conversations of "diversity" and "multiculturalism" made

their way into the university departments of which she was a part, ranks closed, turfs were defended, and curriculum was placed in lockdown to preserve patterns of cultural power and hegemony.

6. Giroux, *On Critical Pedagogy*, 5.

7. hooks, *Teaching to Transgress*, 19.

8. hooks, 22.

9. Henry A. Giroux, *Teachers as Intellectuals: Toward a Critical Pedagogy of Learning* (Granby, MA: Praeger, 1988), 28.

10. Andrew H. Tyner, "Action, Judgment, and Imagination in Hannah Arendt's Thought," *Political Research Quarterly* 70, no. 3 (2017): 530–31.

11. Henry A. Giroux, "Reclaiming the Radical Imagination: Challenging Casino Capitalism's Punishing Factories," Truthout, accessed February 26, 2018, http://www.truth-out.org/opinion/item/21113-disimagination-machines-and-punishing-factories-in-the-age-of-casino-capitalism.

12. Eric J. Weiner, "Critical Pedagogy and the Crisis of Imagination," in Peter McLaren and Joe L. Kincheloe, eds., *Critical Pedagogy: Where Are We Now?* (New York: Lang International Academic, 2007), 65–66.

13. Henry A. Giroux, "The Politics of Disimagination and the Pathologies of Power," Truthout, accessed February 28, 2018, http://www.truth-out.org/new.

14. Giroux, Truthout.

15. Henry A. Giroux, "When Schools Become Dead Zones of the Imagination: A Critical Pedagogy Manifesto," Truthout, accessed February 28, 2018, http://www.truth-out.org/opinion/item/18133-when-schools-become-dead-zones-of-the-imagination-a-critical-pedagogy-manifesto.

16. Giroux.

17. Giroux, "The Politics of Disimagination and the Pathologies of Power."

18. Leonora Tubbs Tisdale, *Prophetic Preaching: A Pastoral Approach* (Louisville, KY: Westminster John Knox, 2010).

19. For this term, see chapter 6 in Richard Eslinger, *The Web of Preaching: New Options In Homiletic Method* (Nashville: Abingdon Press, 2002).

20. Lucy Lind Hogan, "Introduction: Poetics and the Context of Preaching," in Paul Scott Wilson, ed., *The New Interpreter's Handbook of Preaching*, 1st ed., (Nashville: Abingdon Press, 2008), 173.

21. Thomas H. Troeger, *Imagining a Sermon* (Nashville: Abingdon Press, 1990), 26–27.

22. Troeger, 26.

23. Barbara Brown Taylor, *The Preaching Life*, 8th ed., (Cambridge, MS: Cowley, 1993), 44–45.

24. Thomas H. Troeger, "Imagination/Creativity," in Wilson's, *The New Interpreter's Handbook of Preaching*, 192.

25. See the discussion of imagination in Andrea Bieler and Luise Schottroff's, *The Eucharist: Bodies, Bread, & Resurrection* (Minneapolis, MN: Fortress, 2007), 24ff. With thanks to Sam Persons Parkes for conversation around Ricoeur's concept of the function of imagination.

26. Walter Brueggemann, *The Prophetic Imagination* (Philadelphia: Fortress, 1978); Walter Brueggemann, *The Practice of Prophetic Imagination: Preaching an Emancipating Word*, First Edition (Minneapolis, MN: Fortress, 2012).

27. Brueggemann, *The Prophetic Imagination*, 13.

28. Brueggemann, *The Practice of Prophetic Imagination*, 23.

29. Brueggemann, *The Prophetic Imagination*, 16–17.

30. Brueggemann, *The Practice of Prophetic Imagination*, 25.

31. Brueggemann, 25.

32. Brueggemann, 46

33. *Walter Brueggemann, Texts That Linger, Words That Explode: Listening to Prophetic Voices,* ed. Patrick D. Miller (Minneapolis, MN: Fortress, 2000), 44.

34. Kelly Brown Douglas, *Stand Your Ground: Black Bodies and the Justice of God* (Maryknoll, NY: Orbis, 2015), 225.

35. Douglas, 225.

36. Brueggemann, *The Prophetic Imagination*, 13.

37. Kenyatta R. Gilbert, *The Journey and Promise of African American Preaching* (Minneapolis, MN: Fortress, 2011), 62–63. Here I should note the prominence of "conscientization" as a central action of Katie Geneva Cannon's womanist pedagogy. See especially her essay "Metalogues and Dialogues: Teaching the Womanist Idea" in Katie's *Canon: Womanism and the Soul of Black Community* (New York: Continuum, 2003), 136–43.

38. Giroux, "Henry A. Giroux: Reclaiming the Radical Imagination."

39. Giroux, emphasis mine.

40. Henry A. Giroux, *The Public in Peril: Trump and the Menace of American Authoritarianism*, 1st ed., (New York: Routledge, 2017), 252.

41. Giroux, 252.

42. Brueggemann, *The Prophetic Imagination*, 13.

43. Otis Moss III, *Blue Note Preaching in a Post-Soul World: Finding Hope in an Age of Despair* (Louisville, KY: Westminster John Knox, 2015).

44. Moss III, 13.

45. Brian K. Blount, ed., *Can I Get a Witness?: Reading Revelation through African American Culture* (Louisville, KY: Westminster John Knox Press, 2005), 64.

46. Blount, 65.

47. Paul Scott Wilson, *Setting Words on Fire: Putting God at the Center of the Sermon* (Nashville: Abingdon Press, 2008), 1.

48. Wilson, 2. Here I admit to some differences with Wilson in what is properly called "theology of preaching." As a fundamental commitment of my theology of preaching, I do not believe that listeners "hear God speak" through preaching. In response to authoritarianism, I believe this continues to be a dangerous theological commitment. While in preaching I certainly make room for the Holy Spirit to provide fresh address to listeners, I firmly back away from the certainty that listeners hear God speak. And I do not see Wilson as consistent in this commitment through the book. cf. 82–83. I will have more to say about preaching and authority in the next chapter.

49. Wilson, 78.

50. Wilson, 83.

51. Giroux, "Henry A. Giroux: When Schools Become Dead Zones of the Imagination."

Chapter 4

1. bell hooks, *Teaching to Transgress: Education as the Practice of Freedom* (New York: Routledge, 1994), 165.

2. Theodor W. Adorno, *The Psychological Technique of Martin Luther Thomas' Radio Addresses* (Stanford, CA: Stanford University Press, 2000).

3. Adorno, 4.

4. See Adorno, ch. 1.

5. Kyle Eugene Brooks, "'Streets Is Watching': Black Religious Leadership and the Public Sphere" (conference paper), 2018, 1.

6. Brooks draws from Houston Baker, Max Weber, and Roxanne Mountford in accounting for how charismatic leadership is constructed in power relations that account for both gender and race. He problematizes these in some significant ways.

7. hooks, *Teaching to Transgress*, 185.

8. hooks, 195.

9. Henry A. Giroux, "When Schools Become Dead Zones of the Imagination: A Critical Pedagogy Manifesto," Truthout, accessed February 28, 2018, http://www.truth-out.org/opin ion/item/18133-when-schools-become-dead-zones-of-the-imagination-a-critical-pedagogy -manifesto.

10. Fred Craddock, *As One Without Authority*, rev. ed., (St. Louis, MO: Chalice Press, 2001). Originally published in 1971.

11. Thomas G. Long, *The Witness of Preaching*, 3rd ed., (Louisville, KY: Westminster John Knox Press, 2016).

12. Paulo Freire, P*edagogy of the Oppressed* (New York: Continuum, 2000), 39.

13. John S. McClure, *The Roundtable Pulpit: Where Leadership & Preaching Meet* (Nashville: Abingdon Press, 1995); John S. McClure, *Other-Wise Preaching: A Postmodern Ethic for Homiletics* (St. Louis, MO: Chalice, 2001); Robert Stephen Reid, ed., S*low of Speech and Unclean Lips: Contemporary Images of Preaching Identity* (Eugene, OR: Wipf & Stock, 2010); O. Wesley Allen, John McClure, and Ronald J. Allen, eds., *Under the Oak Tree: The Church as Community of Conversation in a Conflicted and Pluralistic World* (Eugene, OR: Cascade, 2013).

14. Lucy Atkinson Rose, *Sharing the Word: Preaching in the Roundtable Church* (Louisville, KY: Westminster John Knox, 1997); O. Wesley Allen, *The Homiletic of All Believers: A Conversational Approach to Proclamation and Preaching* (Louisville, KY: Westminster John Knox, 2005); Ronald J. Allen and O. Wesley Allen Jr., *The Sermon without End: A Conversational Approach to Preaching* (Nashville: Abingdon Press, 2015).

15. Kwok Pui-lan, "Postcolonial Preaching in Intercultural Contexts," *Homiletic* (Online) 40, no. 1 (2015): 18.

16. Pui-lan, 21.

17. Giroux and Robbins, *The Giroux Reader*, 60.

18. Giroux and Robbins, *The Giroux Reader*, 60.

19. Giroux and Robbins, 61.19. Henry A. Giroux, *Fugitive Cultures: Race, Violence, and Youth* (New York: Routledge, 1996), 19–20.

20. Richard W. Voelz, *Youthful Preaching: Strengthening the Relationship between Youth, Adults, and Preaching* (Eugene, OR: Cascade, 2016).

21. Anna Carter Florence, *Preaching as Testimony* (Louisville, KY: Westminster John Knox, 2007).

22. Hannah Spector, "Cultivating the Ethical Imagination in Education: Perspectives from Three Public Intellectuals.," *Review of Education, Pedagogy & Cultural Studies* 39, no. 1 (January 2017): 48.

23. Gail R. O'Day, "Preaching as an Act of Friendship: Plain Speaking as a Sign of the Kingdom," *Journal for Preachers* 28, no. 4 (2005): 15.

24. O'Day, 16.

25. O'Day, 16.

26. O'Day, 18.

27. O'Day, 19.

28. O'Day, 19.

29. Cornel West, *Democracy Matters: Winning the Fight Against Imperialism* (New York: Penguin, 2004), 16.

30. West, 16-17.

31. hooks, *Teaching to Transgress*, 198.

32. Brian K. Blount, "Jesus as Teacher: Boundary Breaking in Mark's Gospel and Today's Church," *Interpretation* 70, no. 2 (April 2016): 184, https://doi.org/10.1177/0020964315622997.

33. Blount, 186.

34. Blount, 191.

35. Henry A. Giroux, *Theory and Resistance in Education: Towards a Pedagogy for the Opposition*, 2nd ed. (Westport, CT: Praeger, 2001), 21.

36. Frank A. Thomas and Henry H. Mitchell, *They Like to Never Quit Praisin' God: The Role of Celebration in Preaching*, Revised, updated ed. (Cleveland, OH: Pilgrim, 2013).

37. Eugene L. Lowry, T*he Homiletical Plot, Expanded Edition: The Sermon as Narrative Art Form*, Expanded, Subsequent edition (Louisville, KY: Westminster John Knox, 2000).

38. Paul Scott Wilson, *The Four Pages of the Sermon: A Guide to Biblical Preaching*, Reprint edition (Nashville: Abingdon Press, 1999). The "four page" sermon finds its shape from a theological hermeneutic of Scripture that moves through a series of steps: "trouble in the text," "trouble in the world," "grace in the text," and "grace in the world."

Chapter 5

1. From Parker Palmer (*The Grace of Great Things: Reclaiming the Sacred in Knowing, Teaching, and Learning*) as quoted by bell hooks in *Teaching Critical Thinking: Practical Wisdom* (New York: Routledge, 2009), 149.

2. Adapted from Sharon Salzberg, "Your Three Feet of Influence." July 14, 2017 blog. On Being. https://onbeing.org/blog/sharon-salzberg-your-three-feet-of-influence/.

3. Brian K. Blount, *Invasion of the Dead: Preaching Resurrection* (Louisville, KY: Westminster John Knox Press, 2014).

4. Nick Tabor, "No Slouch," *The Paris Review* (blog), April 7, 2015, https://www.theparis review.org/blog/2015/04/07/no-slouch/.

CPSIA information can be obtained
at www.ICGtesting.com
Printed in the USA
LVHW012022200619
621901LV00005B/7